THE
Birder's Guide
VANCOUVER  ISLAND

THE
Birder's Guide
VANCOUVER  ISLAND

A Walking Guide to Bird Watching Sites

KEITH TAYLOR

STELLER
press limited

Revised fifth edition
First published in 1983

Published by Steller Press Limited
   1 - 4335 West 10th Avenue
   Vancouver, British Columbia
   V6R 2H6

Canadian Cataloguing in Publication Data
Taylor, K. (Keith),
   A birder's guide to Vancouver Island

   (Steller guides)
   2 ed. Rev.
   includes index
   ISBN 1-894143-03-5

   1. Birding sites—British Columbia—Vancouver Island—
Guidebooks. 2. Bird watching—British Columbia—Vancouver
Island—Guidebooks. 3. Vancouver Island (B.C.)—Guidebooks.
I. Title II. Series
QL685.5.B7T39 1999 598'.07'2347112 C99-901127-8

Printed in Canada

PREFACE

This is the fifth revision of this guide since its introduction in 1983. The first two books were more like annotated lists than actual birdfinding guides. With increased knowledge, the information contained within their pages was reduced to easy-to-read bar-graphs and placed onto a completely new Vancouver Island checklist. The guides that followed contained several pages which listed the records of Vancouver Island vagrant and accidental birds by date and place which, it was hoped, would be an easy reference for local birders. This accidental species list has been omitted in this revision as the occurrence of these species can be more easily referenced by referring to the accidental and vagrant symbols on the Vancouver Island checklist.

With the ever-burgeoning popularity of birding comes a multitude of new and inexperienced birders. Unusual sightings of rare birds of this group should be increasingly more difficult to have accepted, but it seems the opposite is true. The acceptance of records has become notorious with single observer sightings even being added to checklists without hypothetical status. Photographs or confirmation of a species by at least four respected birders should be required before a record is accepted (and even then misidentifications have taken place in the province lately, made known when experts have examined photographs). The accompanying Vancouver Island checklist has an abundance of questionable records which reflects the number of unconfirmed sightings.

To limit unconfirmed records, birders are encouraged to strengthen communication amongst themselves as well as documenting more rarities on film. If you find a vagrant anywhere on Vancouver Island, please drive to the nearest phone and report the sighting immediately to the **Victoria Rare Bird Alert (250-592-3381)** for confirmation. Please follow the instructions to phone others who "hotline" the sighting (just leaving a message on the tape may result in the recording not being heard for the remainder of the day). This will benefit the recording of rarities as well as birder's lists. Also telephone the Victoria Rare Bird Alert and the new **Nanaimo Rare Bird Alert (250-390-3029)** and the **Vancouver Rare Bird Alert (604-737-3074 and enter 4)** for up-to-date information on rare birds.

My particular gratitude is extended to the following people who helped with regions of Vancouver Island: Derrick Marven for Duncan; Wayne Campbell, Adrian Dorst, Aurora Paterson and Dave Hatler for Pacific Rim National Park, Bruce Whittington and Sandy Ruer for Port

Alberni; Howard Telosky and Robert Catchpole for Campbell River; Phil Capes and the Comox-Strathcona Natural History Society for Courtenay; and Steve Baillie for Nanaimo. The staff of the Provincial Museum's Vertebrate Zoology Division were, as always, most helpful.

The friendships of old and new friends helped to update information in the Victoria area: Vic and Peggy Goodwill, Ron Satterfield, Alan MacLeod, Hank Van der Pol, Christopher Sandham, Tim Zurowski, Bryan Gates, Charles Harper, Barbara Begg, and all members of the Victoria Natural History Society.

This book is dedicated to the American Birding Association who have done so much to help foster public appreciation of birds and their vital role in the environment—and who have promoted recreational birding with their continuous contribution to the development of bird identification.

CONTENTS

INTRODUCTION

Lying just off the southern coast of mainland British Columbia is Vancouver Island, 400 kilometers in length and varying in width between the east and west of her coasts. On the southern end is the Saanich Peninsula. Among the hills spotted with bright yellow broom, golden-orange California poppies red-barked arbutus, twisted, knarled Garry oak and towering Douglas-firs you will find homes nestled and sun-soaked on a summer's day. This is Victoria, undoubtedly the best birdfinding city in Canada.

Vancouver Island, the largest island in the eastern Pacific, lies west of Vancouver, parallel to the main coast of British Columbia. The spine of the Island is a range of granite peaks and alpine glaciers that rise to the highest peaks, Golden Hinde (2188 m) and Elkhorne Mountain (2179 m) in Strathcona Park. Eighty percent of this Island stands above 150 meters. On the eastern seaboard lies a narrow low-lying strip of land, the Southeast Coastal Lowlands, a sector of the Georgia Depression eco-region that includes the lower mainland surrounding Vancouver. Here the topography, climate, habitats and avifauna differ greatly from the Island's interior and the west coast. Most of the Island's population lives along the eastern seaboard with few people living on the west coast or interior of the Island, an exciting concept for backcountry explorers. Within Vancouver Island's boundaries lies some of the most photogenic countryside, which could compete with any of the most scenic areas of the planet!

The topography and the prevailing winds from the Pacific Ocean create wet and dry regimes between both coasts: Western mountain slopes hold a huge, irregular strip of wet coniferous forest, while eastern slopes hold semi-arid forests of Garry oak and arbutus with large patches of yellow grasses and cactus-covered, rocky crests.

The journey is a fascinating experience, taking you through the whole spectrum of habitats found throughout this coastal island from sea level to over 10,000 feet in elevation. Nowhere in the world can one watch birds in such an idyllic and spectacular environment, virtually everything from vast swathes of unbroken, verdant forests to jagged, snow-encrusted peaks; from shallow, reed fringed wetlands to turquoise-coloured alpine lakes; from coastal fjords notched and scalloped by countless bays to flower-strewn meadows, from a citadel of mountain woodlands laced with cool, shady canyons to endless dunes basked in warm sunshine.

Many visitors will restrict their birding to Southern Vancouver Island or possibly venture further north throughout the Southeast Coastal Lowlands. All of the bird species that inhabit the Island will be found in this limited area (except pelagic species and the alpine specialities). The text is most comprehensive for this region where the Island's avifauna is concentrated. A trip to Pacific Rim National Park (Tofino or Ucluelet) in the fall is necessary for those wishing a pelagic trip. At any time of the year one will find the scenery and beaches exquisite. The west coast fjords are as spectacular as those of Norway, Chile or New Zealand.

Vancouver Island is a veritable treasure trove of natural wonders, a living natural history museum. Yearly list totals at Victoria reach 235-245 species with big day totals of 135 in early May. Canada's highest Christmas counts have been made in Victoria with 145-152 species. Late spring (May through mid-June) is the best time for the first-time visitor to the region as the weather is at its best and all of the breeding species are singing. Although there are no endemics, birdlife is prolific here with some 392 species recorded, including some of the world's most beautiful and exotic—incredible birds from the large, prehistoric-looking Brandt's Cormorant to the iridescent and diminutive Anna's Hummingbird.

While most American birders come exclusively to list the locally introduced Sky Lark, there are many focal points for Canadian birders looking for specialities of the windswept Pacific coast. Names to entice the mind of any birder: Yellow-billed Loon, Buller's Shearwater, White-tailed Ptarmigan, California Quail, Wandering Tattler, Surfbird, Rock Sandpiper, South Polar Skua, Heermann's Gull, Marbled Murrelet, Cassin's Auklet, Tufted Puffin, Black Swift, Anna's Hummingbird, Red-breasted Sapsucker, Bushtit, Bewick's Wren, Black-throated Gray Warbler, Townsend's Warbler and Black-headed Grosbeak. For foreign birders there is a vast array of species in a tremendous array of colour and shape that will not fail to compete for attention. Flashes of colour will announce hummingbirds, sapsuckers, swallows, jays, waxwings, vireos, warblers, tanagers, grosbeaks, crossbills, and finches. Even a novice birder (not knowing songs and calls) should see 150 species in a three week trip.

Vancouver Island is blessed with an assortment of provincial, national and regional parks strategically located for thoroughly satisfying flora and fauna experiences. There are many of these diverse and exquisite reserves ranging in size from less than one to over several thousand hectares, yielding unlimited birding opportunities—a veritable feast of ornithological riches!

Vancouver Island has a well-maintained highway and road network covering hundreds of kilometers. Many of the better birding areas can be reached by paved roads with excellent roadside birding opportunities. Those wishing to visit the west coast, however, will find limited access on paved roads. Adventurous types looking for solitude may drive the numerous gravel logging roads that form a network of thousands of kilometers over all of the Island's interior, although birders should be aware that some of these roads are private and may require permission.

HOW TO USE THIS BOOK—BIRDING

The main purpose of this guide is to help the independent birder to locate the best places to find all of the regularly occurring species on Vancouver Island, especially the specialties—"A self-made tour for the independent birder". No attempt is made to list all places to bird, but included are samples of those areas where rare, hard-to-find, or specialties occur, especially along the Southeast Coastal Lowlands.

A quick inspection of the book will show that it is divided into several trips along loop routes through the better birding areas, via the shortest distances possible. Each loop-trip has a designated starting point where the kilometerage is indicated as (0.0). Each point of interest or importance thereafter will be followed by the kilometerage from the starting point and the last point mentioned. Starting points change occasionally en route so that you may join the loop, or change to other loops, where you wish.

The maps supplied are generally to scale, however city streets are exaggerated to show detail or simplified for the ease of visual aid. With the directions in this guide and a copy of the "British Columbia Recreational Atlas" finding locations will be easy.

Helpful Icons:

Driving Directions   Where to Find Birds   Bird Listings

A complete Vancouver Island checklist is found in the back of this guide, with bar graphs. A quick inspection of this checklist (along with the National Geographic's *Field Guide to Birds of North America* colour-coded range maps showing the seasonal distribution of birds) will give you all of the information of seasonal occurrence and relative abundance of the avifauna on Vancouver Island. Outstanding birding spots are given headings. If you are in a hurry, stop only at those places so indicated. If you are looking for a particular species, simply look for the species you desire in the index, then find it listed in the text under the locales it should be found. Then consult the checklist and bar graphs to see what your chances are of finding it (its relative abundance in that area), and its seasonal occurrence (does it occur in that month?).

For example: a quick inspection of the the National Geographic's guide will show that the Rock Sandpiper occurs coastally in winter, the checklists and bar graphs tell you that the Rock Sandpiper is local or rare and can be found rarely from mid-July, usually from mid-October through early May, rarely mid-May.

Column 2 on the checklist shows the species recorded on the southwest coast (Jordan River to Port Renfrew) . For Northeastern Vancouver Island, use Column 1 on the checklist noting the differences mentioned in the Eastern and Northeastern Vancouver Island subsections in the Regions – Specialties section. For those birding the East Coast biogeoclimatic zone or birding the Southeast Coastal Lowlands north of Nanaimo use Column 3 on the checklist, checking the footnotes under each subsection in the Regions - Specialties section for the variables in status occuring there.

The common names and order in this guide follows the National Geographic Society's Field Guide to the Birds of North America. Thayer's and Iceland Gulls, both occuring in B C, are occasionally noted separately, but treated as a single species in this guide as there is a distinct possibility of future lumping.

BIRDING

Of the 468 species of birds found in British Columbia, 300 are known to breed in the province Vancouver Island's list has grown to 392. The following occur only as rare or local winter migrants and are quite rare outside of the winter months: Yellow-billed Loon, Clark's Grebe, Emperor Goose, Tufted Duck, Rock Sandpiper, Glaucous Gull, Snowy Owl, Brambling, and Common Redpoll. A further 85 are strictly accidental. Many waterbirds that winter coastally leave in early to late April and move into the interior (or to the Arctic) to breed. (also see How to Use this Book, page 3, and the Checklist at the back of this book).

Birding is best during the cooler early morning hours of summer. The dawn chorus is certainly the best time to find those less common species while they sing. During the winter birds often join into mixed species flocks, feeding together in small groups. Squeeking and pishing is an excellent way of attracting birds for closer views, as well as using the taped songs and calls on a *Field Guide to Western Bird Songs* which work very well on nocturnal species, especially owls.

TIME TO BIRD WATCH

The species you desire to see will determine the best season to visit. Simply consult the bar graphs in the back of this book for this information. For those who need many species spread over the entire year, the best all-around birding is during late April and early May when there is an overlapping of winter and summer birds, plus the spring migrants in full colour. However, the greatest number of rare and accidental species are usually found during the fall migration (September - late November). Late spring (May through mid-June) is a very good time for first-time visitors to this region as the weather is at its best and all of the breeding species are singing. Shorebirds begin to return in late June, although are not prolific in species until mid-August and September. Early summer (late June-July) is the dullest season, but is still rewarding.

If you are in an area during a Christmas count (coastal counts produce 135-150 species) you have a better chance of finding uncommon species pin-pointed during the count and rarities are often produced. The rare Rock Sandpiper is best looked for during the winter months. For pelagic birding, you must arrive in early September.

SUGGESTED REFERENCE MATERIAL

A Birders' Guide to British Columbia, by Keith Taylor, Steller Press (1998)

Field Guide to the Birds of North America, 3rd Edition, by National Geographic Society (1999);

Bntish Columbia Recreational Atlas 2nd Edition (1990)

Field Guide to Western Bird Songs, Cornell Laboratory of Ornithology with Roger T. Peterson, Houghton Mifflin (1992);

Vancouver Island Traveller, by Sandy Bryson, Windham Bay Press, Box 3428 Juneau, Alaska 99803.

ADDITIONAL READING

The Birds of British Columbia Vol. 1, 2 and 3, by R.W. Campbell et al, (1990)

The Naturalists Guide to the Victoria Region, Victoria Natural History Society, P.O. Box 5220, Station B., Victoria, B.C, V8R 6N4

PESTS

Infectious ticks that may carry Lyme Disease or "Rocky Mountain Fever", though rare, can be picked up in brushy areas. These are best avoided by staying on paths and roadways and using insect sprays. Check yourself and remove any ticks immediately. Ticks are a minor problem in Bntish Columbia.

Mosquitoes and blackflies are seldom intolerable on Vancouver Island. You will find mosquitoes to be non-existant or of moderate annoyance in the twilight hours and after dark around marshes or other wet areas. These biting insects are at their worse in June; cover your skin with light clothing and wear a deet repellent. If you are camping, be sure to have "no-see-em" screening on your tent to keep out gnats, especially on the west coast. Mosquito coils or a campfire will keep mosquitoes away when they emerge in the evening. Mosquitoes do not carry any diseases in Canada.

There are poisonous snakes in British Columbia (as there are almost everywhere) so just use common sense and a little caution. Pacific Rattlesnakes are frequently observed in talus and other rock debris areas of the Okanagan.

REGIONS OF VANCOUVER ISLAND

GEOGRAPHY AND CLIMATE

British Columbia's topography varies significantly and may be divided into ten separate eco-regions. Vancouver Island lies in only three of these eco-regions, the Georgia Depression, the Northeast Pacific Ocean, and the Humid Maritime Highlands.

Northeast Pacific Ocean or Pelagic Waters

The oceanic portion of the province is divided into the cooler Alaska current, reaching the northern Queen Charlotte Islands in summer, and the warmer California current, reaching northern Vancouver Island during summer.

Organized pelagic birding trips during the fall off Vancouver Island produce most of the predictable, but exciting species that occur in our waters (see Pelagics pages 18). Pelagic birds are rarely or impossible to see from shore and and a seaworthy boat capable of voyaging 50 kilometers offshore is required. An individual will find that hiring such a vessel will be very expensive indeed, requiring a reservation on an organized trip, or using one of the many ferries plying the B.C. coast. The ferries, however, will produce only a fractional number of species (see M. V. Coho mini-pelagic trip page 20). As access to this habitat is limited by season, the distance travelled offshore, and by the number of trips available, serious pelagic birders will find that such rare species as Laysan Albatross, Short-tailed Albatross, Mottled Petrel, Parakeet Auklet, and possibly even Murphy's Petrel are virtually unattainable in Canada.

If you are planning a pelagic trip in the Pacific Northwest, a half-days drive to Westport in Washington State will give you more opportunities to find unusual pelagics; with more frequent trips seasonally, and by the greater distance travelled offshore. For further information, directions, trip schedules and prices, contact:

T.R. Wahl
3041 Eldridge
Bellingham, WA 98225
Tel: 206-733-8255

For Vancouver Island Pelagic tours see Pacific Rim National Park page 108.

GEORGIA DEPRESSION

The Georgia Depression is a large basin containing the East Coast of Vancouver Island and its low-lying strip known as the Southeast Coastal Lowlands and the "Lower Mainland", the coastal lowlands surrounding the city of Vancouver which stretch north to include the Sunshine Coast and eastward along the Fraser Valley.

Although the Georgia Depression is in the Humid Maritime Highlands Eco division (see following pages), it is distinguished from the adjacent wet coast forests and high mountains by an expansive, fertile, marshy alluvial floodplain—the Fraser Delta (and other adjacent lowlands). This interesting coastal plain holds a juxtaposition of varied habitats including drier deciduous forests of arbutus and garry oak communities, drier extensive mixed forests of red alder, black cottonwood, bigleaf maple, western red-cedar and Douglas-fir, urban parks and agricultural communities, urban development, open sandy shore, rocky coastlines, picturesque lagoons, huge intertidal mudflats, freshwater marshes and saltwater marshes

Human impact is evident almost everywhere with a population of well over three million inhabitants. The "Lower Mainland" and the Saanich Peninsula on adjacent Vancouver Island, although containing most of the urbanized land in the province, have many excellent birding sites. The concentrated birding in the region by numerous experienced people has produced most of the province's most exciting accidental species.

Many bird species are most common or best looked for here than elsewhere in the province: Black-crowned Night-Heron, Green Heron, Cattle Egret (rare late fall) Trumpeter Swan and Tundra Swan (winter), Mute Swan, Snow Goose (winter), Brant (spring), Eurasian Wigeon (winter), Black Scoter (mainly winter), White-winged Scoter, Surf Scoter, Harlequin Duck, shorebirds (see below) Heermann's Gull, Little Gull (rare), Mew Gull, Thayer's Gull (fall-winter) Western Gull, Glaucous-winged Gull, Common Tern (fall), Caspian Tern (summer), Common Murre, Pigeon Guillemot, Marbled Murrelet, Ancient Murrelet (Victoria-fall & winter), Rhinoceros Auklet, Tufted Puffin (Vancouver Island-summer), Mountain Quail (Victoria-exterpated), Band-tailed Pigeon, Barn Owl Western Screech-Owl, Anna's Hummingbird (Victoria), Tropical Kingbird (rare– late fall), Ash-throated Flycatcher (rare), Pacific-slope Flycatcher, Sky Lark (Victoria-local), Purple Martin (Vancouver Island-local) Northwestern Crow, Chestnut-backed Chickadee, Bushtit, Bewick's Wren, Crested Myna (Vancouver-local),

Hutton's Vireo, Black-throated Gray Warbler, Spotted Towhee, Golden-crowned Sparrow (migration, winter), Western Tanager and House Finch.

Migration of shorebirds is quite spectacular! The Fraser Delta supports huge intertidal mudflats and other wetland habitats—as such it has an unparalleled variety of shorebirds along its nutrient-rich shores. The sewage treatment settling ponds at Iona Island are internationally recognized as one of the world's best sites for shorebirds; Eurasian vagrants occur with regularity in late summer, through the fall months. American Avocet, Black-necked Stilt, Snowy Plover, Marbled Godwit, Bar-tailed Godwit, Hudsonian Godwit, Far Eastern Curlew, Willet, Spotted Redshank, Terek Sandpiper, Stilt Sandpiper, Red Knot, Curlew Sandpiper, White-rumped Sandpiper, Baird's Sandpiper, Little Stint, Temminck's Stint, Red-necked Stint, Spoonbill Sandpiper, Sharp-tailed Sandpiper, Ruff, Upland Sandpiper, and Buff-breasted Sandpiper are among the specialities or rarest of shorebirds that have appeared in the Georgia Depression. Both species of golden-plover (Pacific and American) and Semipalmated Sandpiper are recorded in numbers annually.

Black Oystercatcher, Wandering Tattler, Black Turnstone, Surfbird, and Rock Sandpiper are shorebirds that associate with rocky shorelines—although found locally in Vancouver—are more easily located on Vancouver Island.

The Georgia Depression is also a major flyway for a wealth of migrant waterfowl and continues to be of international importance as a wintering area with huge annual concentrations Many loons, grebes, and duck species that summered and breed in the interior (or the Arctic) are found to winter along the rich marine shores or neighbouring unfrozen agricultural fields, marshes, lakes and pools. The Fraser Delta in particular is winter home to tens of thousands of waterfowl including a large proportion of the world's Greater Snow Geese population, some 20,000 individuals. Littoral species such as wintering Pacific Loon, Red-throated Loon, Western Grebe, Red-necked Grebe, Horned Grebe, Eared Grebe, Double-crested Cormorant, Brandt's Cormorant and Pelagic Cormorant, and wintering Greater White-fronted Geese (uncommon), Gadwall, Green-winged Teal, American Wigeon, Northern Pintail, Northern Shoveler, Ruddy Duck, Wood Duck, Canvasback, Redhead, Ring-necked Duck, Tufted Duck (rare & regular), Greater Scaup, Lesser Scaup, Oldsquaw, Barrow's Goldeneye, Common Goldeneye, Bufflehead and Red-breasted Merganser are expected.

The Georgia Depression has the best climate in Canada, basically a

Mediterranean climate of moderately dry, warm springs between the months of March and June, with dry, sunny summers between the months of July and late October. The Georgia Depression lies in the lee of the Vancouver Island and Olympic Peninsula Ranges. The subsequent rainshadow created by these mountains produces drier conditions than the adjacent coastal areas. Summer temperatures range from cool nights of 60°F to midday highs of 70°F. to 85°F., rarely hotter. Winters are wet with endless drizzle and cloud cover, temperatures are usually above freezing with little snowfall at sea level. Temperatures range between 35°F. and 50°F.

Southeast Coastal Lowlands

The Southeast Coastal Lowlands (Georgia Depression in part) consists of a narrow strip of land (much below 500') along the east coast of Vancouver Island from Orveas Bay (Sooke) in the south, to Campbell River in the north. The lowlands also include the Gulf Islands and an isolated lowland area around Port Alberni. A long "finger" reaches inland to include Cowichan Lake.

The Southeast Coastal Lowlands are unique possessing the only prevalent agricultural lands and extensive human habitation on the Island. A multitude of estuarine areas provide "old deltas" containing large tracts of deciduous forests. Alder and cottonwoods along watercourses on these deltas are paramount for breeding Red-eyed Vireos. The dominant forests are of mixed second-growth with small remnant stands of prime Douglas-fir. Drier deciduous forests of garry oak and arbutus communities are usually found on isolated rocky hill tops. Fresh water marshes are scattered in the low-lying coastal strip.

The Southeast Coastal Lowlands has the driest maritime climate and harbours the greatest diversity of avifauna on the Island with many species unique to, or found most commonly in this region:

Pied-billed Grebe – winters most commonly SVI and to north in winter

+ Eared Grebe
• American Bittern R
* Tundra Swan R
+ Mute Swan
* Canada Goose (breeding mainly here)

+ Purple Martin L (estuarine pilings)
** Tree Swallow
** Violet-green Swallow
+ Bank Swallow R
** Cliff Swallow
** Barn Swallow
* Bushtit
  Brown Creeper

Snow Goose U-R
*+ Wood Duck
 + American Black Duck R
Blue-winged Teal
Cinnamon Teal
*+ Northern Shoveler
*+ Gadwall
*+ Eurasian Wigeon
*+ Canvasback
*+ Redhead R
Ring-necked Duck
 + Lesser Scaup
*+ Ruddy Duck
Turkey Vulture
Northern Harrier
Cooper's Hawk
Rough-legged Hawk R
American Kestrel
*+ California Quail
 * Ring-necked Pheasant
 + Anna's Hummingbird L
Willow Flycatcher
 + Sky Lark L
Horned Lark
 + Black-headed Grosbeak
Chipping Sparrow
 + Vesper Sparrow R
 + Swamp Sparrow R
 * White-throated Sparrow R
Harris's Sparrow R
Western Meadowlark

Bewick's Wren
 + House Wren
 * Marsh Wren
Virginia Rail
Sora
 * American Coot—winters
most commonly SVI
Solitary Sandpiper
Sharp-tailed Sandpiper R
 + Stilt Sandpiper R
 + Buff-breasted Sandpiper R
 + Franklin's Gull R
 + Little Gull R
 + Common Tern
Rock Dove
 + Mourning Dove
*+ Barn Owl R
Short-eared Owl
Northern Saw-whet Owl
Bohemian Waxwing
(regular northeast coast)
Northern Shrike
Red-eyed Vireo
Black-throated Gray Warbler
Yellow-headed Blackbird R
 + Rusty Blackbird R
 * Bullock's Oriole U. L
House Finch
House Sparrow
Spotted Towhee (only
abundant in this zone)

Key to Symbols

*	mainly north to Comox	+ found most commonly on
•	found most commonly at Nanimo	southern Vancouver Island.
**	local on west coast	

R Rare   U Uncommon   L Local

The Southeast Coastal Lowlands may be divided into three sub-regions—Southern Vancouver Island (SVI), Orveas Bay north to Nanaimo; the Northern Lowlands, north to Campbell River; and the Alberni Lowlands surrounding Port Alberni.

Southern Vancouver Island

Southern Vancouver Island has the least amount of precipitation on the Island, is mild in winter, generally above freezing with frequent drizzle. In summer the region is moderately warm with little rainfall in June through October. Victoria has the mildest climate in Canada, very similar to that experienced in San Francisco, California.

A journey outside this region is not required as all of the species that inhabit Vancouver Island may be located in this relatively small area, the exception being pelagics and alpine specialties North America's only introduced population of Sky Larks are restricted to the Saanich Peninsula. The numbers have declined to about 150 individuals but are still easy to locate in their limited range. However, with rapid development and changing agricultural practices, one severe winter could eliminate this species from the list of North American breeding avifauna.

Other species that are sought most often by visiting birders include California Quail, Anna's Hummingbird, alcids,"rock" shorebirds, Bushtit and Red-breasted Sapsucker.

Three species, Green Heron, Red-eyed Vireo and Black-headed Grosbeak are found most easily in the Duncan area with a fourth species, Northern Saw-whet Owl, found most commonly along the Southeast Coastal Lowland north of the Malahat. American Bittern is usually a rare winter visitor and most easily found locally at Nanaimo where it is resident. California Gull, Western Gull, Heermann's Gull and Rhinoceros Auklet are most numerous on Southern Vancouver Island (as compared to the northeast coast—see also West Coast column 1 of the checklist).

The best shorebirding along the east coast is found on Southern Vancouver Island.

Northern-Southeast Coastal Lowlands

Summers are much like those of Southern Vancouver Island with little rainfall. The climate, predictably, is much cooler in winter with more frequent snows. This, and other factors, has the effect on a few of the resident lowland specialties decreasing in population northward including: Ring-necked Pheasant, California Quail (north to Comox), Bushtit and Marsh Wren. Summer residents such as House Wren and Black-headed Grosbeak are much less numerous. A number of dabbling ducks are also scarce, among them Northern Shoveler, Gadwall, Eurasian Wigeon, Canvasback and Ruddy Duck.

Though still rare, Bohemian Waxwing and Pine Grosbeak are found more easily in this region, especially during invasion years. Red-breasted Sapsucker are more common and found readily at low elevations along the coast all year. On Southern Vancouver Island, they are usually found inland in summer at higher elevations. Black Scoter and Black Swift are common in this region during summer. Unlike Southern Vancouver Island, Sharp-shinned Hawk are prevalent in summer as are Northern Harrier, Herring Gull, Bonaparte's Gull and Common Loon. Golden-crowned Sparrow and White-crowned Sparrow are not as common during the winter months and Brandt's Cormorant is mainly found during the winter.

Alberni Lowlands

Port Albemi lies within an isolated area of the Southeast Coastal Lowlands known as the Alberni Lowlands. The status of birds in the Alberni Lowlands is homogenous with that of the northern sector of the Southeast Coastal Lowlands except that the isolation and close proximity to Western Vancouver Island limits the number of "lowland specialties". Those absent or rare in this region include California Quail, Sora, Cliff Swallow, Red-eyed Vireo, Black-headed Grosbeak and Chipping Sparrow. House Sparrow are uncommon residents. Southeast Coastal Lowland ducks that are absent, local, or very rare include Gadwall, Northern Shoveler, Canvasback, Redhead and Black Scoter. Harlequin Duck, Oldsquaw, White-winged Scoter and Red-breasted Merganser are rare at the head of the inlet. The speciality species is the "Green Pheasant", a race of the Ring-necked Pheasant.

The avifauna on the Southeast Coastal Lowlands is predominantly homogenous except for the noted seasonal and other minor variables that occur.

EASTERN VANCOUVER ISLAND (east coast zone)

The Eastern Vancouver Island biogeoclimatic zone consists mainly of highlands (although there are few alpine areas). The exception is a small area of West Coast Zone along Buttle Lake. There are few settlements, the access to most of this region is along logging roads.

Elevation regulates seasonal temperatures and snowfall with few species present at higher elevations during the winter months. In summer, the region receives little rainfall. The forests are of drier maritime with Douglas-fir the dominant tree species. Valleys, logging slash and roadways are fringed with alders.

The division line between East and Western Vancouver Islands biogeoclimatic zones restricts such species as Western Wood-Pewee and Western Tanager to the drier East Coast, sharing distribution with the Southeast Coast Lowlands. (Hammond's Flycatcher also fits into this category but has tiny populations in limited colonies scattered in the Western zone). Other species that share this distribution but are found less commonly in the Eastern zone than the Southeast Coastal Lowlands, but also found thinly distributed on the West Coast, include Willow Flycatcher, Red-breasted Nuthatch, Brown Creeper, Cassin's Vireo, Yellow Warbler and Common Yellowthroat.

Although almost confined to the West Coast as a breeding species, small populations of Hermit Thrush nest on isolated higher mountains within the East Coast zone with Mount Brenton (west of Chemainus) and Butler Peak (in the Nanaimo Lakes region) having the most southeasterly records during the breeding season. Hermits almost certainly breed further south along the edge of the West Coast zone, especially on the higher Weeks lake Plateau. The Hermit Thrush has not been confirmed within the Victoria checklist area in June or July.

Three species may be found most easily in the East Coast zone than elsewhere on the Island: Northern Pygmy-Owl and Blue Grouse (both sharing distribution with the West Coast and thinly distributed on the Southeast Coastal Lowlands) and Red-breasted Sapsucker (sharing distribution with the Southeast Coastal Lowlands, especially to the north, and thinly distributed on the West Coast) .

Northeastern Vancouver Island

The avifauna in this sector is very similar to that on the West Coast except for the variables noted in the Eastern Vancouver Island section above. Dabbling ducks share status with the West Coast, except Northern Shoveler and Ring-necked Duck which are more prevalent during migrations. The shoveler occasionally winters and the Ring-necked Duck may be present during the summer months. Red-winged Blackbird, Brewer's Blackbird and Barred Owl may be found, although the blackbirds are scarce in winter. Large flocks of Sandhill Crane are most prevalent on Vancouver Island in this sector during September. Sharp-shinned Hawk are found during the summer months and Brandt's Cormorant seldom during winter. Ruby-crowned Kinglet breed uncommonly throughout this region.

During the fall months, pelagics invade Johnstone Straits. The most notable of these are both Fork-tailed Storm-Petrel and Leach's Storm-Petrel.

HUMID MARITIME HIGHLANDS (coast and mountains)

Along the Pacific Coast of British Columbia, the Coast Mountains, Nass Basin, and Nass Ranges hold a huge, irregular strip of wet coniferous forest dominated by Douglas-fir, western red-cedar, yellow-cedar, western hemlock, Sitka spruce and amabilis fir. The region includes the windward side of these mountains, the west coast of Vancouver Island, and all of the Queen Charlotte Islands. Here, among the world's densest coniferous forests are towering monolithic Douglas-firs. High overhead, sunlight penetrates the canopy in a cathedral manner, filtering beams of silky-light across their immense trunks. Along watercourses and in disturbed (burned, logged) areas the successional species are broad-leafed maple and red alder. These wet forests are akin to the wet forests of the Southern Interior Mountains and neither are noted for having a richness in bird species in the conifer belts. A few species associated with these forests are Band-tailed Pigeon, Western Screech-Owl, Red-breasted Sapsucker, Pacific-slope Flycatcher, Steller's Jay, Northwestern Crow, Chestnut-backed Chickadee, Winter Wren, Varied Thrush, and Townsend's Warbler. The coastal mountains have large areas of alpine (most of which is inaccessible) that hold the characteristic birds of this region.

The littoral waters of the coastal straits, inlets, shores, and the adjacent lowlands are rich in species however. The coastline is a major flyway for a plentitude of species including a wide variety of waterbirds and shorebirds to a mixture of passerines. As this habitat is representative of the Georgia Depression, it is treated more fully under that heading.

The climate of this region at lower elevations is quite temperate, as temperatures are influenced by the relative proximity to the sea. As one accends the spectacular peaks to alpine, temperatures drop accordingly. Temperatures along the coast are generally above freezing in winter months with little snowfall, midday summer temperatures are seldom warmer than 75°F. to 85°F. with cool nights. Precipitation and cloud cover are abundant for much of year.

WESTERN VANCOUVER ISLAND

Contrast conditions prevail on the Island's west coast which gets the full force of Pacific storms. Rugged, wind-swept islands, long, deeply indented coastline with dramatic fjords, surf-swept headlands and golden-sand beaches are constantly battered by the cold waters of the Pacific. Her stark mountain ranges and savage coastlines, shrouded in rain and mist for most of the year—all are enhanced by the peculiar quality of the light, which lends an ethereal beauty to the landscape.

The open coastline can be cool, wet with frequent fog, even in the summer months. Average temperature readings at Tofino are: August 14°C. (58° F.) and in January 4°C. (39°F.). Yearly precipitation, which is primarily rain at sea level and snow at higher elevations, is approx. 250 cm. annually. While rain gear is standard equipment for life on the west coast, there are many sunny days in summer.

Western Vancouver Island, with the wettest maritime climate, has markedly different vegetation than its drier east coast. On land, the west coast conifer rainforest is predominate, harbouring cathedral-like forests containing ancient giants, their huge limbs festooned with exquisite epiphytic mosses and ferns. Intermediate areas are of red alder and roadways are fringed with this species which are paramount for breeding Warbling Vireo. Isolated disturbed areas, especially slash from logging in various stages of regeneration, add variety to birdlife, particularly at lower elevations. The few available bogs offer habitat for Common Yellowthroat and these bogs and damp brushy areas support Yellow Warbler and rarely Willow Flycatcher.

Bio-geoclimatically, the whole region encompassing the West Coast zone is quite similar with the status of most bird species being homogenous although some seasonal variations occur from north to south.

Many species of birds found in the East Coast zone of Vancouver Island are lacking in the West Coast zone—no avifauna is restricted to the West Coast zone except pelagics and the alpine specialties. The high mountainous interior has many alpine ridges harbouring the alpine species. The interior of the west coast along its many logging roads is especially low in avifaunal diversity -in winter virtually sterile. A few species are found more readily on the west coast during summer, however, when most travellers visit Pacific Rim National Park. Pacific Loon, Red-throated Loon, Black-legged Kittiwake, Western Gull, Tufted Puffin and breeding Fox Sparrow and Hermit Thrush.

Organized pelagic trips are few and usually limited to the fall months (see Pacific Rim National Park section).

Despite the fewer species to be found along the west coast, many very rare birds have been, and are yet, to be discovered!

ALPINE

Alpine scenery is spectacular! Vistas present fantastic views of the surrounding precipitous crags, distant valleys, and emerald alpine lakes. At dawn, mountain peaks often poke through the early morning clouds, resembling islands in a white sea.

Most of Vancouver Island's alpine areas are found within the West Coast zone, with the exception of Mount Arrowsmith which is found on the east coast west of Parksville. Alpine is widespread on the highest peaks, most of which are inaccessible. The few areas that are attainable are on gravel or logging roads, at skiing developments and at communication installations. Characteristic birds of the alpine include White-tailed Ptarmigan and Gray Jay, which is found over all of Vancouver Island above 2,500 feet, Three-toed Woodpecker are rare in the subalpine. Breeding American Pipit are local or rare and Gray-crowned Rosy Finch are very uncommon but to be expected at Mount Washington Ski Area. The three most accessible alpine areas are Mount Arrowsmith , Mount Washington Ski Area and Flower Bridge Trail in Strathcona Park.

Strenuous hiking is required to reach the beautiful alpine ridges that harbour the Ptarmigan.

MAP 1—Alpine Zones

COMMON, CONSPICUOUS ROADSIDE SPECIES

The following partial list of species may be seen en route to destinations, commonly viewed flying across roads, in fields, on roadside poles and wires, or in roadside pools and marshes.

Great Blue Heron
Canada Goose
Mallard
Killdeer
Glaucous-winged Gull
Red-tailed Hawk
Ring-necked Pheasant
Rock Dove
Rufous Hummingbird
Belted Kingfisher
Northern Flicker
Downy Woodpecker
Violet-green Swallow

Barn Swallow
Steller's Jay
Northwestern Crow
Common Raven
American Robin
European Starling
Savannah Sparow
Song Sparow
Red-winged Blackbird
Brewer's Blackbird
House Sparrow
House Finch
American Goldfinch

PELAGICS

Albatross
Short-tailed Albatross R
Black-footed Albatross
Laysan Albatross R

Shearwaters and Petrels
Northern Fulmar
Flesh-footed Shearwater
Sooty Shearwater
Short-tailed Shearwater
Pink-footed Shearwater
Buller's Shearwater
Black-vented Shearwater R

Gadfly Petrels
Mottled Petrel R

Storm-Petrels
Leach's Storm-Petrel
Fork-tailed Storm-Petrel

Frigatebirds
Magnificent Frigatebird Acc

Phalaropes
Red-necked Phalarope
Red Phalarope

Tropicbirds
Red-tailed Tropicbird Acc

Skuas, Gulls, Terns
South Polar Skua
Pomarine Jaeger
Parasitic Jaeger
Long-tailed Jaeger
Black-legged Kittiwake
Sabine's Gull
Arctic Tern

Alcids
Thick-billed Murre R
Xantus's Murrelet Acc
Cassin's Auklet
Parakeet Auklet R
Horned Puffin R
Tufted Puffin

MAP 2—Road Systems of Vancouver Island

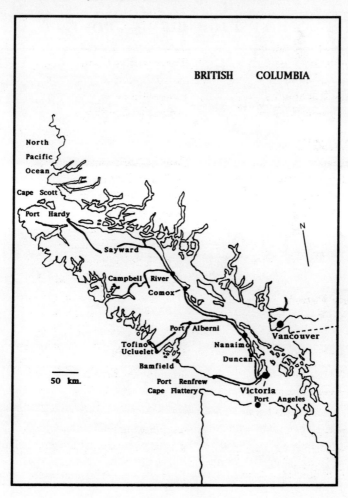

FERRY ROUTES TO VICTORIA

M. V. Coho Mini-pelagic Trip

Although Victoria does not face the open Pacific, a number of pelagic species find their way up Juan de Fuca Strait to this area. They can be sighted from such promontories as Clover Point, Ten-Mile Point and Albert Head and from leisure craft, commercial fishing vessels, and from aboard the M V Coho. Most pelagic species are seen during the fall migration period. Their occurrence this far up the Strait of Juan de Fuca may be weather-related, the birds being either blown in during storms or lost in heavy fogs.

MAP 3—COHO PELAGIC BIRDING ROUTE

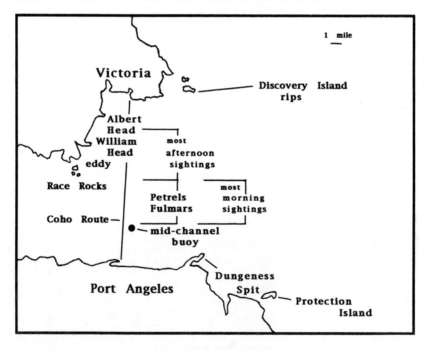

The best time to see pelagics is from mid-September to late November, with November showing peak numbers of individuals and species. The most frequently encountered pelagic species are Fork-tailed Storm-Petrel, Sooty Shearwater, Northern

Fulmar, Red-necked Phalarope, Parasitic Jaeger and Ancient Murrelet. Littoral species that are abundant or regularly seen from the ferries in season include Common Murre, Rhinoceros Auklet, Marbled Murrelet, Pigeon Guillemot, and our three species of cormorant as well as water-fowl and gulls. Rarely seen pelagics include Leach's Storm-Petrel, Cassin's Auklet (irregular during summer in El Nino years) and Tufted Puffin. Short-tailed Shearwater (very rare) and Red Phalarope (uncommon) occasionally occur in numbers.

The M.V Coho ferry leaves Victoria from 430 Belleville Street and travels through the Juan de Fuca Strait to Port Angeles. Departure times and frequencies vary seasonally. Same-day return trips can only be made from mid-March through late November. Crossing time is 1 hour 35 minutes each way. The viewer should dress warmly and stand directly at the bow where the wind is deflected overhead.

Storm-Petrels and Fulmars are most often seen in the area of swell south of Race Rocks and north of the mid-channel buoy. Most pelagics are encountered here on the morning trips to Port Angeles; on the afternoon trips most are seen north of Race Rocks closer to Victoria. For those with wider interests, the usual marine mammals seen from the ferry are Harbour Seal, Dall's and Harbour Porpoise, occasionally Killer Whales, Steller's and California Sea Lions and rarely Elephant Seal.

Mainland to Vancouver Island Ferry Trips

Reaching the shores of the Saanich Peninsula requires a luxury cruise of over an hour and a half out of the Port of Tsawwassen near Ladner (south of Vancouver) and the route is well designated by road signs. The ferry lands at Swartz Bay, 32 kilometers north of Victoria.

The first half of the ferry trip is crossing the Georgia Strait and there is poor birding until Active Pass is reached. During winter and migrations hundreds of Pacific Loon, Bonaparte's Gull and Brandt's Cormorant feed in the churning waters. Northwestern Crow dot the scenery. Lesser numbers of Common Murre, Pigeon Guillemot, Marbled Murrelet and Bald Eagle are seen regularly throughout the year. Lucky birders will spot Black Oystercatcher on the rocks on the waterline, the rare Little Gull, or a Parasitic Jaeger or two in fall.

The islands on either side are but the beginning of many to be passed. Now the ocean is filled with scattered islands, the San Juan

Islands. Varying in size from San Juan embracing 56 square miles, to chains of tide-washed rocks, their rough, rocky shore-lines are cut deeply by long, steep-walled fjords glaciated in years past. Their numerous steep hills are crowned with stands of Douglas-fir, red-barked arbutus, and big-leaf Maples. Rain falls constantly in winter months, but summers are arid and large patches of dry, yellow grasses cover the rocky crests interspersed with small clumps of prickly cactus.

Those using the Anacortes Ferry will experience a similar crossing as above, with a good chance of seeing Ancient Murrelet in season. Those crossing to Nanaimo will see little (a slim chance of Fork-tailed Storm-Petrel) with no islets passed on the crossing.

Arrival at Victoria

Victoria lies nestled between sea and mountains in the extreme south-western corner of British Columbia in the Georgia Depression eco-region.

The fantastic birding opportunities in and around Victoria is a direct consequence of the highly varied topography combined with an extraordinary diversity of climatic conditions and habitats. Indeed, there have been 354 species of avifauna recorded to date. This interesting region is a must on anyone's itinerary to B.C.

Victoria, with over 500,000 inhabitants, is British Columbia's second largest city. Nevertheless, a greater proportion of the province's accidental and vagrant bird records are made at the excellent birding sites dotted around the city and budget birders will find that these birding sites are easily accessed by public transit buses. A number of species are most common or best looked for on the Saanich Peninsula than elsewhere in the province (see Georgia Depression) while others are only found in this region of British Columbia, and one, the introduced Sky Lark, nowhere else in North America except the outer Aleutians.

SAANICH PENINSULA LOOP (VICTORIA)

Tsawwassen Ferry Terminal to Swartz Bay

We begin our tour at the Tsawwassen Ferry Terminal in Vancouver, follow the signs for the Tsawwassen Ferry Terminal from Highways 10, 17 or 99. Before, or after leaving the ferry terminal, pull over onto the wide shoulder of the road (anywhere you see something of interest) along the three kilometer stretch of man-made spit. There are large rafts of sea ducks present during the winter months and tens of thousands of Dunlin on the vast mudflats at the head of the bay. Loons, grebes, cormorants, and gull species are well represented. Heermann's Gull are seen fairly regularly as post-breeding wanderers in late summer and fall. A small population of Brant winter on offshore waters, while numbers can be seen during the spring migration period. The rock jettys at the terminal often have Harlequin Duck, Black-bellied Plover, Greater Yellowlegs, Black Turnstone and occasionally Sanderling in winter. A lucky observer may see a Parasitic Jaeger harrassing a flock of Common Tern in the fall. A Lapland Longspur or Snow Bunting may frequent the weedy patches between the drift-logs on the beaches along the causeway during the late fall.

Swartz Bay to Deep Cove

Swartz Bay: (00 0 km.) After leaving the ferry from Tsawwassen drive (1.2 km.), turning right at the traffic lights onto Wain Road (sign for Deep Cove) After (2.3 km.) (3.5 km.) continue past West Saanich Road and turn right onto Madrona Drive (2.1 km) (5.6 km) After driving an additional (0.3 km) (5.9 km) turn left onto Setchell Road; drive to the terminus (0.2 km) (6.1 km.).

Deep Cove

The north end of the Saanich Peninsula is a fairly regular area for migrant and wintering Yellow-billed Loon (rare). They are found especially during late January through February, recorded here many years with as many as three sighted at once. Scope the offshore waters, especially the less sheltered areas. Many Common Loon and Pacific Loon will be present. Common Murre, Marbled Murrelet and Pigeon Guillemot will be seen. A few Barrow's Goldeneye forage along the shoreline. Returning to Madrona Drive, turn right. After driving (0.6 km.) (6.7 km.) park at the foot of Cromar Road. The beach access allows one more opportunity to scope further for Yellow-billed Loon. Continue on Madrona Drive for an additional (0.4 km) (7.1 km.), turning right onto Norris Road and park. Scope once more for Yellow-billed Loon.

PLACE NAMES OF THE SAANICH PENINSULA LOOP

1 Deep Cove
2 Patricia Bay
3 Sidney Island
4 Victoria International Airport
5 Bazan Bay
6 Wallace Drive (bulb fields)
7 Thompson Place
8 Saanichton Spit
9 Island View Road—Martindale Road
10 Cordova Bay
11 Blenkinsop Lake
12 Mount Douglas Park
13 Ten Mile Point
14 University Grounds—Mount Tolmie
15 Cattle Point- Upland Park
16 Victoria Golf Course—McMicking Point
17 Clover Point
18 Beacon Hill Park
19 Ogden Point Breakwall
20 Swan Lake Nature Sanctuary
21 Elk Lake—Jennings Lane—Beaver Lake
22 Quick's Bottom
23 Interurban—Courtland Flats
24 Hasting's Flats
25 Francis King Regional Park
26 Munn Road
27 Esquimalt Lagoon
28 Witty's Lagoon
29 Durrance Lake Owling Loop
30 Goldstream Provincial Park
31 Town and Country Mall

Map 4—Saanich Peninsula Loop

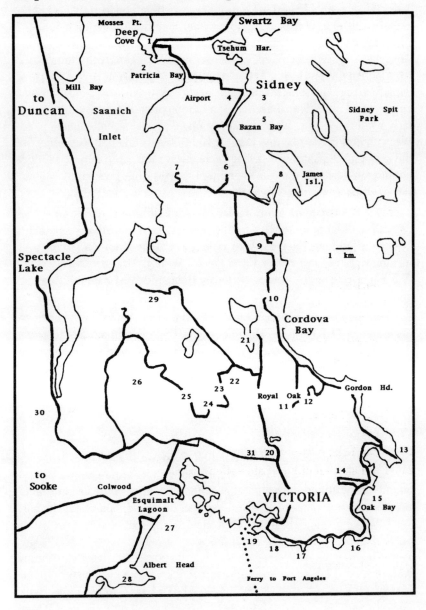

The brushy margins along Madrona Drive and Norris Road in this residential area afford an excellent opportunity to find lowland birds during the winter months. Among them Chestnut-backed Chickadee, Red-breasted Nuthatch, Brown Creeper, Bewick's Wren, Winter Wren, Golden-crowned Kinglet, Ruby-crowned Kinglet, American Robin, Varied Thrush, Spotted Towhee, Fox Sparrow, Song Sparrow, Golden-crowned Sparrow, Dark-eyed Junco, Purple Finch and House Finch. The abundant berry crops provide food for the regularly wintering Cedar Waxwing (uncommon). The rare Bohemian Waxwing has been recorded here. A Blue Jay has taken up residence in the area for the past three or four years, most likely an escapee, as it has not migrated as would a true vagrant. However, Blue Jays have become rare, regular winter visitors to the Victoria region during the 1990's.

Continue on Madrona Drive for an additional (0.3 km.) (7.4 km.) and park for the beach access to further scope for Yellow-billed Loon. Retrace your route back along Madrona Drive, turning right on Downy Road (0.5 km) (7.9 km.). After driving (1.6 km.) (9.5 km), park on the corner of Downy Road and West Saanich Road and scan the garry oaks for birds.

Turn right onto West Saanich Road (00.0 km.). At (3.2 km.) park beside Patricia Bay on the shoulder of West Saanich Road. At the northern corner of the bay a small raft of Black Scoter should be found in the winter months. Many other wintering waterfowl will be found with Barrow's Goldeneye, Surf Scoter, White-winged Scoter and a few Eared Grebe scattered over the bay. Yellow-billed Loon have been recorded.

Deep Bay to Sidney

Continue along West Saanich Road turning left onto Mills Road (1.2 km.) (4.4 km). If you wish, continue along West Saanich to Willingdon Road at the southwest corner of the airport for a possible nesting pair of Red-eyed Vireo in the deciduous woods during June. While driving Mills Road the Victoria International Airport will be on your right. Scan the perimeter fence and isolated trees for Merlin and Peregrine Falcon; occasionally American Kestrels, Northern Harrier and Northern Shrike may be present. After (1.9 km) (6.5 km.) turn right onto McDonald Park—hence Henry Roads. At (0.5 km) (7.0 km.) turn right on Galaran Road. After (0.5 km) (7.5 km.) turn left onto Beacon Avenue for downtown Sidney. After (1.3 km.) (8.8 km.) turn left onto Seaport Avenue for the little foot ferry to Sidney Spit Provincial Park. The ferry leaves from the end of the government wharf at the foot of Beacon Avenue, 0.2 km from Seapon Avenue. Scan for alcids and waterfowl off the government pier. Oldsquaw are especially numerous in winter.

Sidney Spit Provincial Park

Sidney Island provides the best shorebirding on southern Vancouver Island. Several habitats include sandy beaches, pebble areas, mudflats and rocky stretches. Near the end of the spit is an area with pilings that floods during high tides. Here, at lower tides, Black Oystercatcher, Ruddy Turnstone and Black Turnstone congregate. On the surrounding beaches one will find Black-bellied Plover (occasionally hundreds), Pacific Golden-Plover (rare), American Golden-Plover (uncommon), Semipalmated Plover, Whimbrel (uncommon), Red Knot (rare-regular), Sanderling and Baird's Sandpiper (uncommon). The rare Buff-breasted Sandpiper may be regular in August. To bird the most productive mudflats of Sidney Lagoon requires an hours walk around the edge of the lagoon to the opposite shore from where the ferry lands. Try to get a passing boater to give you a lift across the short stretch of water. At low tide you may wade.

On the mudflats you may locate some of the above species plus "peep" including thousands of Western Sandpiper, Least Sandpiper and a few Semipalmated Sandpiper. Long-billed Dowitcher, Short-billed Dowitcher, Lesser Yellowlegs, Greater Yellowlegs and Pectoral Sandpiper may be encountered. Rarities such as Stilt Sandpiper, Marbled Godwit, Long-billed Curlew and two hypothetical records of Bristle-thighed Curlew exist. On the island at the head of the lagoon is a Bald Eagle nest.

Resting on the beaches are Common Tern, (rarely Caspian Tern), Bonaparte's Gull, Heermann's Gull, California Gull, Mew Gull and Glaucous-winged Gull. Birding is fair in the woods with Black-throated Gray Warbler in the more deciduous tracts and House Wren around the campsites. Interesting are the large herds of introduced Fallow Deer, numbers of Common Peafowl, a few Wild Turkey (dependent on feeders and "uncountable") and other exotics.

On the crossing to Sidney Island you will have excellent views of Rhinoceros Auklet, Pigeon Guillemot and Marbled Murrelet. Very rarely Tufted Puffin are seen from the small breeding colony at Mandarte Island, the white-washed rock to the east of Sidney Spit. Red-necked Phalarope may also be seen during the crossing.

Sidney to Bazan Bay & Victoria International Airport

(00.0 km.) Return to Beacon Avenue and immediately turn left onto First Street and continue along Ocean Avenue, passing the Anacortes Ferry Terminal. At (0.8 km.) turn left onto Marvette Place. After (0.3 km.) (1.1 km.) turn left into Tulista Park. An excellent spot to scope Bazan Bay. Brant are numerous here in late March and April. At the picnic grounds you may eat and enjoy the spectacular scenery of the San Juan Islands while watching for Bald Eagle above the tree tops. In winter, the islands are usually enshrouded in a gray mist.

Return to Marvette Place (now Lockside Drive) and turn left. There are many pull overs to further check Bazan Bay. After (1.5 km.) (2.6 km.) turn right and follow the Victoria sign, crossing over the highway. Turn right after (0.3 km.) (2.9 km) at the sign for the airport onto Canora Road. After an additional (0.3 km) (3.2 km) keep right for the industrial area and continue on Canora Road to its terminus at the Victoria International Airport (1.4 km.) (4.6 km.). Sky Larks will be found breeding in the short-grass runways in summer. Listen for the long sustained song of liquid notes as the bird hovers high in the air. During periodic years of Snowy Owl invasions this rare owl may be seen from this vantage point. Common Nighthawk dart over the runways on summer evenings.

Victoria International Airport to the Bulb Fields

(00.0 km.) Return back along Canora Road. Turn left at Willingdon-Canora Roads (0.8 km.) (1.3 km), then right at McTavish (0.4 km.) (1.7 km.) and then left at East Saanich Road (0.6 km) (2.3 km.). After (1.3 km.) (3.8 km.) turn left onto Lowe Road which soon changes name to Emard Terrace—then to Amity Road. At (0.7 km.) (4.3 km.) turn right onto Aldous Terrace which changes to Wallace Drive at the Central Saanich border. Stop at (0.7 km.) (5.0 km).

CENTRAL SAANICH BULB FIELDS

The surrounding agricultural bulb fields are most productive throughout the year for Sky Lark, especially the fallow field just north of the large greenhouse complex on East Saanich Road (the next road that runs parallel below to the east). This field is the best site during fall and winter for Western Meadowlark. Please respect this private property and do not walk the fields when the flowers are growing! Many unplanted rows may be walked throughout the year.

Fallow grassy sections may hold a Short-eared Owl during winter with Savannah Sparrow occasionally remaining through winter. This is the best site for Horned Lark which are regular from September through October and, although rare, during winter. Common Snipe winter annually and Ring-necked Pheasant are resident. When the majority of the fields have been left fallow and contain a short, twisted mat of dried weeds, thousands of American Pipits may descend during years of high population or because of favourable weather conditions. Check amongst these large flocks during September and early October as there are three records of Red-throated Pipit and one of Yellow Wagtail. Grasshopper Sparrow has been seen as well. Red-throated Pipits tend to stay hidden in taller vegetation than the American Pipits and are usually flushed before they are seen. Listen for their very high, long drawn-out "speeeeeeh" flight call. A small flock of Mourning Dove winter with individuals through summer. Check the feeder in front of the home at 8503 Ebor Terrace without disturbing the owners (south off Amity Road between Aldous Terrace and Bourne Terrace) where the Mourning Dove flock feeds during winter—a few roost in the neighbouring trees.

Bulb Fields to Thompson Place

An additional site to see Mourning Dove in summer is Thompson Place. Continue on Wallace Drive passing East Saanich Road, then turning right onto Mount Newton Crossroad (00.0 km.). Drive for an additional (2.2 km.) then turn right onto Thompson Place. At (1.6 km.) (3.8 km.) stop at the summit of Mount Newton and listen for the mournful song. House Wren, Olive-sided Flycatcher and Western Tanager (uncommon) will be found.

Thompson Place to Island View Beach

From Thompson Place return to Mt. Newton Crossroad turning left (00.0 km.). Follow Mt. Newton Crossroad, turning right onto the Patricia Bay Highway (Highway 17) (3.5 km.). Those wishing to stay at the KOA campground, proceed across the highway following the KOA. signs to the office (2.3 km) (5.8 km). This is private property—please obey speed signs! The small bay and mudflats at Saanichton Spit adjacent to the KOA campgrounds are excellent birding sites. Only guests of the KOA can access the spit from the campgrounds (see under Island View Beach).

Proceed south along the Patricia Bay Highway, turning left at the traffic lights onto Island View Road (2.3 km.) (5.8 km.), then right onto McHugh Road (1.0 km.) (6.8 km). Turn left on McIntyre (0.4 km.) (7.2 km.) and park at (0.1 km) (7.3 km.) for McIntyre Resevoir.

Island View Road and Beach

The surrounding agricultural fields along Island View Road and those along Martindale Road (the next road to the south) rank among the most important birding sites on the Island and have produced one hundred species of birds in a single winters day. From Island View Road you may search for the species mentioned along Martindale Road (see page 31). Walking the fields is permited but be respectful of crops!

At night, play a tape at the corner of Island View and Puckle Roads to entice a Barn Owl into view, which usually flies past silently to observe the intruder. Watch for the large butterfly-like silhouette.

Check the fallow grassy field on the slope at the corner of McIntyre and McHugh Roads at any season for Sky Lark and Savannah Sparrow. Short-eared Owl and Western Meadowlark are rare in October through the winter months whilst the occasional Northern Harrier is seen quartering the fallow fields during the fall and winter. Lincoln's Sparrow winter in the reed canary grass, especially around McIntyre Reservoir. The resevoir is the best site in Victoria for freshwater shorebirds during late summer and early fall when the water levels are low. Greater Yellowlegs, Lesser Yellowlegs, Solitary Sandpiper (uncommon), Spotted Sandpiper, Western Sandpiper, Least Sandpiper, Baird's Sandpiper (uncommon), Pectoral Sandpiper, Sharp-tailed Sandpiper (rare), Stilt Sandpiper (uncommon-best site), Short-billed Dowitcher, Long-billed Dowitcher (good site) and Wilson's Phalarope (rare) are possible.

Return to Island View Road, turning right (00.0 km.). you may continue driving on Island View Road to its terminus at Island View Beach Regional Park. Park en route at the top of the hill (0.7 km) during the winter months and walk southeast along the dirt farm road approximately (0.3 km.) towards the derilict farm truck. The grasses and manure in the vicinity of the truck attract a few Golden-crowned Sparrow and a Harris's Sparrow has wintered for two years. Onshore at Island View Beach (1.5 km) in winter are thousands of sea ducks and alcids including numerous Oldsquaw, and to the north, close to the boundary with Saanichton Spit, a few Black Scoter. Common Loon, Yellow-billed Loon (rare), Pacific Loon, Red-throated Loon, Red-necked Grebe, Horned Grebe, Eared Grebe (uncommon), Greater Scaup, White-winged Scoter, Surf Scoter, Barrow's Goldeneye (uncommon), Common Goldeneye, Bufflehead, Red-breasted Merganser, Common Murre, Pigeon Guillemot, Marbled Murrelet and Rhinoceros Auklet are regular.

In the abandoned farm fields back of the beach are many hawthorn trees which harbour the odd Northern Shrike during winter. Short-eared Owl are occasionally flushed in early morning hours during October from the grassy areas. Rarities found along the trails include Lewis's Woodpecker, Say's Phoebe and Mountain Bluebird. The weedy fields south of the foot of Island View Road may have numerous sparrows during the winter months with Spotted Towhee, Savannah Sparrow, Song Sparrow, American Tree Sparrow (rare), Dark-eyed Junco, White-crowned Sparrow, Golden-crowned Sparrow and Lincoln's Sparrow at various times. Tree Swallow nest in the man-made nest boxes.

Continue walking north along the beach to gain access to Saanichton Spit one and a half kilometers from the parking lot. The small bay and mudflats at Saanichton Spit are excellent for shorebirds. All of the regularly occuring mudflat species will be encountered. White-faced Ibis, Bar-tailed Godwit, Hudsonian Godwit and Upland Sandpiper have been found. The very small pool near the sewage treatment plant has peeps at high tides providing close views. The offshore navy bouy has all three species of cormorant roosting in summer including Brandt's Cormorant. Often summering Pacific Loon are seen offshore. In winter Northern Shrike are often encountered on the spit and Short-eared Owl in the long grasses during migration in October. This is a good area for waterfowl and alcids which are common offshore. Nesting Common Nighthawk (rare) may be flushed off the spit. Check the firs nearby for Band-tailed Pigeon and the adjacent woodlots for Hutton's Vireo.

Martindale Road

Return to Highway 17 turning left (00.0 km.), then left onto Martindale Road (1.2 km.). After an additional (0.6 km.) (1.8 km) check the lombardy poplars for possible nesting Bullock's Orioles. Look through the thickets in winter along Lockside Drive (especially north along the gravel sector) for Spotted Towhee, Song Sparrow, possibly the rare American Tree Sparrow, Dark-eyed Junco,

Golden-crowned Sparrow, Fox Sparrow and Lincoln's Sparrow. Rarities include Long-eared Owl and the first confirmed Ash-throated Flycatcher.

Martindale is another excellent site for Sky Lark and it will be heard singing high over the fields in summer. After (0.2 km.) (2.0 km) walk across the field along the ditch past the "L" reservoir, visible as a hump to the south. Small flocks of Sky Lark may be flushed from agricultural or short grass fields and especially from the corn stubble behind this reservoir during winter. At this season rains have flooded the lower vegetable fields beside the road. Ducks, mainly American Wigeon, mix with numbers of Mallard and the odd Northern Pintail and Northern Shoveler. Large white shapes contrasting sharply with the black, wet earth materialize into flocks of Trumpeter Swan. Scan these flocks, as they feed on vegetable matter left over from the fall harvest, for one or two Tundra Swan that may be present. Blue-winged Teal and Cinnamon Teal are found during migration.

Many species of raptor are found in the area especially during the winter months with Bald Eagle, Northern Harrier, Sharp-shinned Hawk, Cooper's Hawk, Red-tailed Hawk, Merlin and rarely a Golden Eagle or Rough-legged Hawk. Check the large cotton-woods and telephone poles for Peregrine Falcon which are found feeding upon the wintering waterfowl each year. Gyrfalcon is always a possibility. Check for jessess as falconers often fly (and loose) their birds here!

The flooded fields harbour wintering Black-bellied Plover, Common Snipe, Killdeer and Dunlin. Wet fields in May have produced Semipalmated Plover, Spotted Sandpiper, Western Sandpiper, Least Sandpiper, Pectoral Sandpiper (uncommon), Short-billed Dowitcher, Long-billed Dowitcher and Wilson's Phalarope (rare). Greater Yellowlegs and Lesser Yellowlegs parade sedately in the background.

American Pipit are abundant in the surrounding fields during fall migration with a few remaining in the onion fields for the winter. Horned Lark are uncommon migrants and rare winter visitors. Lapland Longspur are occasionally seen in small flocks during fall, but usually singles are found. The yellow breasts of Western Meadowlark brighten the grasses during the fall and winter while Marsh Wren and Savannah Sparrow are flushed or heard calling in the grassy sections along ditches between Martindale and Island View Roads in winter or summer. Northern Shrike may be encountered. Watch and listen for Ring-necked Pheasant. Bobolink are very rare migrants in the fall months. White-faced Ibis, Prairie Falcon, Loggerhead Shrike,

Yellow Wagtail, Common Grackle and Grasshopper Sparrow are among the rarities recorded here.

Scan the numerous migrating swallows over the fields and along the wires in August and September for Bank Swallow which are rare but regular. In the vicinity will be a large flock of blackbirds containing hundreds of Brewer's Blackbird and Red-winged Blackbird. Scan for the rare but regular Rusty Blackbird in fall and winter. Yellow-headed Blackbird (rare) may be found throughout the year but are found most often in the fall. Brown-headed Cowbird regularly winter in the blackbird flocks.

Martindale Road to Cordova Bay

At (1.0 km) (3.0 km.) turn right onto Welsh Road which turns to Hunt -then Sayward Roads. After an additional (2.8 km.) (5.8 km.) turn left onto Fowler Road which soon changes name to Cordova Bay Road. Check the hawthorns along the drive for Cedar Waxwing, Bohemian Waxwing (very rare), American Robin, Varied Thrush, Ruby-crowned Kinglet, Purple Finch and occasionally Band-tailed Pigeon when the trees are filled with berries in cold weather. At the corner of Fowler and Cordova Bay Roads, check the gravel pit for Northern Rough-winged Swallow that nest there. Continue to Cordova Bay (2.5 km.) (8.3 km.)

Cordova Bay

At the parking lot beside the Seaview Inn is a small park where you may scope Cordova Bay for loons, grebes, alcids and saltwater ducks. Thirty-five or more Eared Grebe winter in the bay annually and should be seen scattered mainly to the southeast. A scope is usually essential to see the steeper forehead, darker ear-coverts, dirty-grey foreneck, upturned bill and "fluffed out" rear body that produces the characteristic profile that will help to identity the distant Eared Grebe from the abundant Horned Grebe.

After driving south (0.4 km) (8.7 km) you may turn right onto Claremont Avenue for an additional (0.2 km.) (8.9 km.). A left turn on Lockside Drive for (0.4 km) (9.3 km.) will bring you to 4950 Lockside Drive where Band-tailed Pigeon regularly visit a feeder each year during the winter months. Also scan the tips of the surrounding Douglas-firs.

(00.0 km.) Proceed along Cordova Bay Road. After (1.1 km.) you will see D'Arcy Lane on your left. If you missed Eared Grebe at the Seaview

Inn, try again from the end of D'Arcy Lane. A raft of Ruddy Duck winters annually on the bay.

Cordova Bay to Blenkinsop Lake and Mount Douglas

Back on Cordova Bay Road continue south for (1.1 km.) (2.2 km.) and turn left at the traffic lights if you wish go proceed along Cordova Bay Road. If you wish to visit Blenkinsop Lake drive straight ahead on Blenkinsop Road for (1.4 km.) (3.6 km), turning right onto Lohbrunner Road, then left on Lockside Drive and park at its terminus. The trail to the lake is good for migrating warblers and resident Downy Woodpecker, Bewick's Wren, Song Sparrow and Spotted Towhee. During summer, small numbers of Black-headed Grosbeak nest along the trail and Yellow Warbler and Common Yellowthroat are numerous.

Check the lake for Wood Duck and rarely Green Heron. A few Marsh Wren sing from the reedy areas.

From the lights at Cordova Bay Road (see above) (00.0 km.) drive south (2.3 km.) and turn right onto Churchill Drive at the corner of Shelbourne Street for Mount Douglas Park. A short walk in the cool, mixed forest along Churchill Drive should produce Pacific-slope Flycatcher, Winter Wren, Cassin's Vireo, Hutton's Vireo, Warbling Vireo, Black-throated Gray Warbler, Townsend's Warbler, Wilson's Warbler and Western Tanager. At the summit watch the open skies for aerial feeders such as swallows and migrant Black Swift and Vaux's Swift which cut across the spectacular vistas on sickle wings. Olive-sided Flycatcher, House Wren and Western Tanager call below on the dry southwest slope. Fortunate birders may find Townsend's Solitaire, vagrant kingbirds during late April or a Lazuli Bunting in early June. In late April 1992 a Hermit Warbler was recorded on the summit and nearby a Hermit x Townsend's Warbler hybrid .

Mount Douglas Park to Ten Mile Point

(00.0 km) As you leave the park, turn left onto Cordova Bay Road for (0.5 km.), then turn right onto Ash Road. After (0.9 km) (1.4 km.) Ash Road changes to Grandview Drive. At (1.1 km.) (2.5 km.) Grandview changes name to Ferndale Road. After (0.3 km.) (2.8 km.) Ferndale Road then changes to Gordon Head Road at the curve. After (0.3 km.) (3.1 km.) turn left onto Arbutus Road. After (1.8 km.) (4.9 km) Rowley Road is on the right. Anna's Hummingbird will be found in the fields at the corners of Arbutus-Rowley-Queenswood Roads.

Ten Mile Point

At (4.9 km.) turn right off Arbutus Road onto Telegraph Bay Road (00.0 km.). Turn left at Sea View Road (0.1 km.), then immediately left at Tudor Avenue (0.1 km.). You are now on a peninsula known as Ten Mile Point. After (0.5 km.) (0.6 km.) watch at the corner of Woodhaven Terrace for Anna's Hummingbird which come to feeders along Woodhaven or along Tudor Avenue. Do not trespass or disturb their owners! After an additional (0.5 km.) (1.1 km) park on the right at the sharp curve along Tudor Avenue. A check of the rocks in the bay, or more often the rocks behind the private residence on the left (east) side of the bay, should produce a Whimbrel or two which winter every year. Anna's Hummingbird visit the feeders at the corner. At (0.3 km.) (1.4 km.) turn right onto Baynes Road, then left at White Rock Street (0.4 km) (1.8 km) to its end (0.2 km.) (2.0 km.).

Haro Straits lie in front of you where Ancient Murrelet winter annually. On a good day thousands stretch to the horizon in their typical single file "string" formations. A scope is usually essential to view the distant birds, but often the birds come close to shore. Look carefully as their heads just break the surface of the water as they dive again. Tides must be just right to find the birds here. If you miss them, try again at another time of day (mid-morning may be best). In this area from December through early February there are many loons, grebes, and sea ducks, especially Oldsquaw which also feed on the euphausiids.

Ten Mile Point to Cadboro Bay

Return to Telegraph Bay Road which soon changes to Cadboro Bay Road (00.0 km.). After driving (0.9 km) you will see Penrhyn Street on your left. At number 2600 the MacKenzie-Grieves have resident Anna's Hummingbirds and, although there are only two records of Costa's Hummingbirds for Victoria, both occurred here. It should be noted that the population of Anna's Hummingbirds has increased greatly in the past few years and the birds can be seen easily at other locations without the need to disturb feeder owners, as was often the case in the past. A further (0.2 km.) (1.1 km.) along Cadboro Bay Road you may turn left onto Killarney Road and park at its terminus with Cadboro Bay (0.2 km.) (1.3 km.). The uncommon Semipalmated Sandpiper is regular on the bay. Walk southwest along the beach in July and August checking through the "peep".

Cadboro Bay to University, Mt. Tolmie and Lansdowne

(00.0 km) Proceed along Cadboro Bay Road, turning left after (0.5 km.) through the Uplands gates onto Beach Drive. For a side trip you may continue along Cadboro Bay Road for an additional (0.2 km), turning right onto Cedar Hill Cross Road for the University of Victoria, Mount Tolmie and Lansdowne School. We will do the side trip first (main loop continued on page 41).

University of Victoria

(00.0 km) From the corner of Cadboro Bay and Cedar Hill Cross Roads proceed west for (0.8 km) and park opposite the west end of Henderson Park. A chip trail leads into the university grounds on the right side of Cedar Hill Cross Road. The usual "rain-forest" species will be found. Walk the chip trail until it curves left and listen for the high, squeaky song of an Anna's Hummingbird. The hummingbirds are common residents in the university's ornamental gardens. At the first "T" junction of two chip trails, take the trail leading to the left, then to the right. Scan the Douglas-firs and arbutus trees surrounding this junction where a reliable Barred Owl roosts throughout the year. The owl sits in plain view at heights of 30'. Back at the first "T" junction, proceed right along the trail to the second "T" junction. In winter, "squeek" the feeding flocks containing Golden-crowned Kinglet and Chestnut-backed Chickadee to attract a Hutton's Vireo. The vireo will appear instantly, peer inquisitively at the intruder and vanish. In early spring and summer the monotonous song drifts through the surrounding woods.

Mount Tolmie Park

Continue west on Cedar Hill Cross Road for an additional (0.8 km.) (1.6 km.), turning left onto Mayfair Dr. at the Mount Tolmie sign.

The comforting warmth of sunlight is seldom felt on the skin while walking the dark trails through the rain-drenched,cathedral-like west coast forests—seeking the sunlit slopes where deciduous arbutus and garry oak communities has always been a delightful alternative—and relinquishing a greater number of rarities!

MAP 5—Mount Tolmie Park

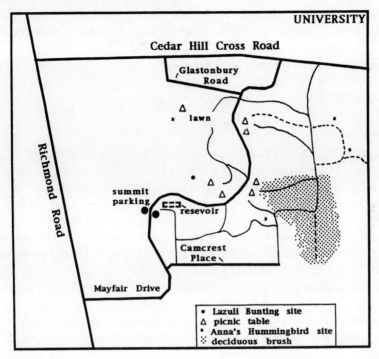

UNIVERSITY

Cedar Hill Cross Road

Glastonbury Road

Richmond Road

△
• lawn

summit parking
resevoir

Camcrest Place

Mayfair Drive

• Lazuli Bunting site
△ picnic table
• Anna's Hummingbird site
∷ deciduous brush

Atop Mount Tolmie, elevated above the surrounding metropolis of Victoria, the pocket-sized morsel of magical Californian-like habitat seems misplaced. Here, among sun-soaked garry oaks, chrome-yellow broom, flaxen grasses, and cadmium-orange California poppies, one can breathe perfumed air amidst magnificent scenic surroundings and bird with great expectations. Over 140 species have been recorded along the excellent network of trails.

Small navigators make big mistakes—birders have learned that they can intercept some of these strays by positioning themselves at strategic points for the possibility of seeing these vagrants. Mount Tolmie is one of these places. As migrant passerines are confronted by southerly low pressure systems bringing adverse weather, "fall-outs" occur. When these ideal conditions exist, the park then becomes attractive to these migrants, the small navigators often seeking the highest point of land—especially when confronted with a water crossing. The prime season for weather systems and migrants to coincide, creating these fall-outs, is during the months of May and early June. At other times, especially during sunny weather, there will be few birds. For visiting birders, the park has a fair selection ot western specialities, for locals it provides the opportunity ot experiencing passerine fall-outs and the chance of locating some wayward vagrant trom the east or south.

Mount Tolmie has had its share of strays over the years. In the last three years there have been two records of Ash-throated Flycatcher and single records of Magnolia Warbler, Blackpoll Warbler, Tennessee Warbler, Indigo Bunting, Lark Sparrow, Black-throated Sparrow and Smith's Longspur. Both Western Kingbird and Eastern Kingbird are fairly regular with Western Kingbird seen annually. Mount Tolmie boasts as the Island's mecca for Lazuli Bunting, recorded during May and June the last few years. This rarity can appear each spring for a few years, then mysteriously disappear just as quickly for a number of years before reappearing. Mount Tolmie also boasts as one of the better sites to see Anna's Hummingbirds in the "wild" in Canada with four males holding territories.

Mount Tolmie can be accessed from either Cedar Hill Cross or Richmond Roads, just south and west of the University of Victoria. From Cedar Hill Cross Road, turn left at the park sign onto Mayfair Drive and drive to the summit. Starting from the summit parking lot, walk east towards the large cement reservoir used for water storage. A wide chip trail starts off from the south side leading downhill and soon a branch trail should be followed to the left. During their April migration period, Townsend's Solitaires are regularly seen in this area. Usually a soft "eek" betrays their presence as they call from the tips of the Douglas-firs in the neighbouring properties. A dozen can be seen in a good year, with six on an average year. A male Anna's Hummingbird holds territory in the short garry oaks along the left side of the path where the path reaches a "T" junction at the bottom of the hill. This individual is only present during the height of breeding. A Smith's Longspur was present in the rocky, short grass areas of the hill during mid-September of 1990.

A short jog to the left, then right at the bottom of the hill will bring you to an area of moist deciduous scrub where the usual breeding species are Bewick's Wren, Spotted Towhee and Song Sparrow. All lurk quietly next to fallen logs or in shady recesses in the tangled vegetation. The odd House Wren (rare in this sector of the city) has been seen in late April-early May with a pair nesting. It is in this area that a pair of

Least Flycatcher nested in 1970 and the first confirmed record of Tennessee Warbler was made for the checklist area. Long-eared Owl have been found roosting in the Douglas-firs or dense brush close to the homes while a pair of Cooper's Hawk nest in the vicinity.

Mount Tolmie may be one of the better sites for Western Wood-Pewee which are regular migrants during mid-May through early June and rarely non-breeding individuals can be found through summer. Hermit Thrush and Lincoln's Sparrow are very common migrants during their migration "windows". An Ash-throated Flycatcher was seen briefly in September of 1992. This sector of the park can be alive with flycatchers, vireos, warblers, grosbeaks, tanagers, and sparrows during drop-outs. Downy Woodpecker, Olive-sided Flycatcher, Hammond's Flycatcher, Pacific-slope Flycatcher, Chestnut-backed Chickadee, Bushtit, Red-breasted Nuthatch, Brown Creeper, Winter Wren, Golden-crowned Kinglet, Ruby-crowned Kinglet, Swainson's Thrush (uncommon), American Robin, Varied Thrush, Cedar Waxwing, Cassin's Vireo, Warbling Vireo, Red-eyed Vireo (rare), Orange-Crowned Warbler, Yellow Warbler, Yellow-rumped Warbler, Black-throated Gray Warbler, Townsend's Warbler, MacGillivray's Warbler (uncommon), Wilson's Warbler, Common Yellowthroat, Fox Sparrow, Golden-crowned Sparrow, White-crowned Sparrow, Dark-eyed Junco, Brown-headed Cowbird, Purple Finch and Red Crossbill all occur in season.

A hybrid Townsend's x Hermit Warbler was present during late April 1998, singing a typical Hermit's song. There are only two confirmed records of Hermit Warbler for Vancouver Island—a male in Victoria on Mt. Douglas and a female near Port Alberni (there are other uncon-firmed sightings). Hermit Warblers and their hybrids appear during late April—early May, with an atypical record of a pair, a hybrid male and the female mentioned above, present in June. There are at least four confirmed hybrids. Three of these hybrids mirrored Hermit Warblers except for a wash or patch of yellow present on the upper breast and having slightly more olive upperparts (the Mt. Tolmie and Port Alberni birds were of this type—see illustration on page 38 of Warblers of the Americas). A third present on Mt. Douglas was similar to the illustration in the National Geographic's Field Guide to the Birds of North America, appearing more Townsend's-like with a yellow face.

 Proceed along the chip trail in a northerly direction. Take the first non-chip trail on your right through an area of broom and short garry oaks. Soon you will come to a fork, keep left on the non-chip trail. The garry oak with the heavy dead snag close to the beige home is a "station" for a reliable male Anna's Hummingbird. He can be seen virtually at any time throughout the year, although post-breeding dispersal takes place about mid-July and Anna's Hummingbird but may be difficult to find again until early September. Listen for his high squeaking song. If you are fortunate he will treat you to his display flight, breaking all the laws of aerodynamics. Comical little knob-topped California Quail are common during the summer months, retreating to neighbouring residential backyards during winter. A second unconfirmed Ash-throated Flycatcher was discovered here in late May of 1990.

Follow the path as it turns back towards the west where it will soon rejoin the chip trail. An uncooperative Indigo Bunting was found near this junction in late May 1992 and a Lark Sparrow frequented the area in September 1990. Savannah Sparrow are common migrants among the arid hillsides with the odd Short-eared Owl encountered in grass-clumps during October (Victoria's two summer records come from Mount Tolmie). This is another area where Townsend's Solitaire occur each April and although kingbirds can be found anywhere on Mount Tolmie, they are found here more regularly. Chipping Sparrow breed each year in the vicinity, their streaky juveniles appearing during mid-July.

Follow the chip trail downhill, turning left at the first junction with another chip trail (if you continue straight ahead you can join other trails around the university grounds). This trail will cross over Mayfair Drive that leads up and over Mount Tolmie. The path then turns south and uphill to an area of lawn containing a picnic table. Walk over to the rocks near the picnic table where there is a fantastic vista of the surrounding city lying in a maze of dramatic hills and intervening valleys. The dry hillside above is "the" locality for finding Lazuli Bunting in Victoria. Another "interior" species, Nashville Warbler, has been recorded. American Kestrels are frequently observed sitting on snags in April and September. The surrounding garry oaks always have good numbers of migrant Black-headed Grosbeak and jewel-like Western Tanagers each spring but during drop-outs as many as 50 of each of these species have been recorded in a single morning. Evening Grosbeaks are heard flying over in winter on occasion, while in summer they can be quite common.

Walk the chip trail towards the summit. At the large gravel area walk along the cliff edge checking the blackberry brambles for sparrows in winter. The odd White-throated Sparrow occurs with the Golden-crowned Sparrow, Dark-eyed Junco and House Finch flocks. Winter is usually unchangable on the mountain with few species although Townsend's Solitaire has been recorded.

Back at the summit parking lot, check the rocky areas, especially at the northern edge of the railing where Horned Lark, American Pipit, and a surprising number of Lapland Longspurs forage each autumn. Snow Bunting is a real rarity here! Although the park is not a hawk watching site, raptors can be well represented, silently soaring overhead on still wings. Bald Eagle, Sharp-shinned Hawk, Red-tailed Hawk, and Merlin can be seen fairly regularly especially during migrations. Watch the open skies for aerial feeders such as flocks of swallows as both Black and Vaux's Swift cut across the spectacular vistas on sickle wings at unimaginable speeds during summer as storm fronts pass. Violet-green Swallows nest at man-made nest boxes in the neighbourhood. Diurnal flights of migrating Common Nighthawk are seen from the summit during August as they use the Mount Tolmie-Ten Mile Point corridor and then cross Haro Straits to San Juan Island (many raptors also use this route).

Mount Tolmie to Lansdowne School—back to main loop

From the Summit of Mount Tolmie, drive down the south side along Mayfair Drive to Richmond Road (00.0 km.). Turn left onto Richmond Road, then left onto Lansdowne Road (0.8 km.). Park in the Lansdowne School parking lot, a left turn after an additional (0.2 km.) (1.0 km.). Shorebirds, especially the larger species, inhabit the playing fields before they are flushed by hoards of people. Early in the morning you could find Black-bellied Plover, American Golden-Plover, Whimbrel, Short-billed Dowitcher, Long-billed Dowitcher, Common Snipe, Baird's Sandpiper or Pectoral Sandpiper. Among the rarest species recorded include Upland Sandpiper and Marbled Godwit.

Return to our loop by driving east (a right turn from the school) along Lansdowne Road to Beach Drive (2.7 km.). Kilometerages are taken from the Upland gates.

Cadboro Bay to Loon and Spoon Bays and Cattle Point

After an additional (0.9 km.) (1.4 km.) check for shorebirds at Loon Bay near the Royal Victoria Yacht Club. Greater

Yellowlegs, Short-billed Dowitcher, Western Sandpiper, Least Sandpiper and Semipalmated Sandpiper are regulars. At the foot of Lansdowne Road (0.3 km.) (1.7 km.) park and walk the beach access to Spoon Bay. During fall and winter storms shorebirds find refuge in this bay. The rocks to the right (south) may hold 50 Black Oystercatcher, many Black Turnstone, Surfbird, Dunlin, Black-bellied Plover, Greater Yellowlegs, possibly Rock Sandpiper (rare) or Whimbrel (rare). A scope is necessary for viewing.

Cattle Point and Uplands Park

Continue along Beach Drive. Turn left onto Surrey Road (0.7 km.) (2.4 km.). The small offshore rocks, "rocker rocks", have been the most reliable site to locate Rock Sandpiper (rare) in recent years in January through April. After (0.4 km.) (2.8 km.) turn left for Cattle Point and Uplands Park. Loons, grebes and alcids are common offshore during the winter months and this is an especially good site for Marbled Murrelet and Pigeon Guillemot. Brandt's Cormorant are common on the offshore Chain Islets but seldom close enough to see well. Black Oystercatcher, Black Turnstone and Surfbird are regulars. Parasitic Jaeger are often seen parasitizing Common Tern offshore in September and October. Migrant Lapland Longspur, Snow Bunting (both uncommon) and Horned Lark (regular late September—early October) will be found in the short grass areas.

In the park Bewick's Wren, various sparrows in season, California Quail, Chestnut-backed Chickadee and Bushtit will be found in the scrub along the numerous trails.

Cattle Point to Bowker Creek and Oak Bay

Return to Beach Drive, turning left for an additional (1.6 km.) (4.4 km.) and turn left onto Bowker Avenue. Park at the terminus (0.1 km.) (4.5 km). A walk to the right towards Bowker Creek along the rocky shoreline should produce many "rock shorebirds" especially at low tides early in the day. This is the most reliable area for Surfbird. The Red Knot is rare but has been found on numerous occasions in late September through October. Black-bellied Plover, Greater Yellowlegs, Black Turnstone and Dunlin winter here. Hooded Merganser winter commonly in the bay with many other species of salt-water ducks. Common Tern are always seen resting on the rocks even in those years when numbers are low. This is the site where the earliest arrivals are found in mid-July. During the Bonaparte's Gull migration period check through the flocks feeding along the beaches for a possible Little Gull or Franklin's Gull.

(00.0 km) Return to Beach Drive, turning left for (0.8 km) to Oak Bay. Eurasian Wigeon regularly winter here or at Bowker Creek with the American Wigeon. American Coot, Greater Yellowlegs and Killdeer frequent the small park at the bay during winter. Pied-billed Grebe and Hooded Merganser are among the more common wintering waterrfowl.

Oak Bay to Victoria Golf Course and McMicking Point

Continue along Beach Drive for another (1.6 km.) (2.4 km.) and pull off on the left for the Victoria Golf Course. As the course is private property, birding is only tolerated early in the morning and in late evening which is the best time for birding anyway.

The most productive location is along the waterfront, walking east over the rocky bluff to Gonzales Point. All through the year Brandt's Cormorant should be found among the Pelagic Cormorant and Double-crested Cormorant roosting on the rocks. The thickets of broom and blackberries should be checked for Golden-crowned Sparrow and Fox Sparrow in winter, Lincoln's Sparrow in migration, and Calitornia Quail and House Finch all year. The golf course is best known for the shorebirds that frequent the fairways during fall migration. Both Pacific and American Golden-Plovers are found.

Golden-plovers continue to be incorrectly identified and this has led to controversy over which species is the most frequently observed. In an average year, golden-plovers are usually fairly rare along both coasts of Vancouver Island although juveniles of both species are found in somewhat proportional numbers in the fall (adult Pacific Golden-Plovers are the most prevalent species along the west coast in the spring). The east coast of the Island receives the spoils from the major fall migration of shorebirds which stage on the Fraser Delta's extensive mudflats, where American Golden-Plovers far outnumber the Pacific. During years of high population, or because of unspecified weather conditions, formidable numbers of American Golden-Plovers invade the Fraser Delta. During these times, numbers spill over onto the Island when American Golden-Plovers become uncommon and surpass the Pacific in numbers. Adult golden-plovers are extremely rare along the east coast of the Island in spring (May) when the American is the dominate species. Averaging the populations of both species along the east coast of Vancouver Island over a span of several years, the American outnumbers the Pacific.

Identifying golden-plovers can be a challenge for the inexperienced. The text and illustrations found in Lars Jonsson's Birds of Europe are among the best. The better characteristics for identifying juvenile Pacific Golden-Plovers from the American are: shorter primary projection with three primary tips exposed whereas American shows four; longer legs which project well beyond the tail in flight; big dark eye on a pale background with a dark patch on the rear ear-coverts; warmer overall buff-yellow tones; and the calls. The American gives a clear, somewhat vibrating whistle, "kuee-eep", in flight, while on the ground it gives a "kweep" which is not as sharp as the Pacific's call. The Pacific's is a sharp "chuwit" or softer "kluee."

 Migrant Black-bellied Plover remain through winter and Black Oystercatcher are resident. Occasional species seen during migration are Buff-breasted Sandpiper, Marbled Godwit and very rarely Ruff. Wandering Tattler, Whimbrel, Baird's Sandpiper, Pectoral Sandpiper, Long-billed Dowitcher, Short-billed Dowitcher, Greater Yellowlegs, Killdeer, Black Turnstone, Surfbird and Dunlin are encountered seasonally.

Scan offshore for loons, grebes, alcids, Oldsquaw, Harlequin Duck, Common Tern, Heermann's Gull, Red-necked Phalarope and Parasitic Jaeger in season. Short-eared Owl may be flushed from the rocky bluff in October. Horned Lark, American Pipit, Lapland Longspur and Snow Bunting are found during migrations. Mountain Bluebird are rare but have been found many years during November. Many rare migrants, including Chestnut-collared Longspur, have rested here before crossing the straits.

After an additional (0.5 km.) (2.9 km.) pull over on the left for McMicking Point—Hood Lane Sewer Outfall. A walk along the old cement pipe and adjacent peninsula could produce a Wandering Tattler in May or from mid-July through early October. The Victoria Golf Course, McMicking Point and Holland Point are the most productive sites for this sought-after species. The sewer outfall has been closed, but several common species of gull are still seen roosting on the rocks. Pigeon Guillemot are seen in the channel and Harlequin Duck are resident. Caspian Tern may be encountered regularly in late summer. Numerous resident Pelagic Cormorant and Double-crested Cormorant winter and all three cormorant species will be seen sitting together on

the rocks for comparison. Bald Eagle sit on the posts on offshore Trial
Island (rarely, Snowy Owl on the crests) with basking Harbour Seals
along the shore.

McMicking Point to Clover Point

Proceed along Beach Drive. After (0.9 km.) (3.8 km.) turn left
onto King George Terrace which changes name to Crescent
Road at (0.3 km.) (4.1 km.) then Ross Street at (0.5 km.) (4.6 km.). After
(0.2 km.) (4.8 km.) turn left at St. Charles Street, then right at Dallas
Road (0.1 km) (4.9 km.). After (1.2 km.) (6.1 km.) turn left onto Clover
Point. Red-breasted Sapsucker frequent the pines in Ross Bay Cemetery
when arctic fronts bring extremely cold winter weather.

Clover Point

When speaking of birding in Victoria, Clover Point comes with
the second breath. A chapter could be written on the possibilities alone—Emperor Goose, Tufted Duck, Ross's Gull, Black-headed
Gull, Slaty-backed Gull, Black-necked Stilt, Bar-tailed Godwit, Elegant
Tern, Ruff, Horned Puffin and Northern Hawk-Owl are a few of the best
records that have been made. The point is but the beginning of a park
running along a bluff abutting the sea and overlooking the snow-capped
domes of the mountainous Olympic Peninsula. Vistas are impressive!

Clover Point offers the birder "armchair" birding. Just sit in your car
and watch the birds fly by on blustery fall days. Scan the rocks for Black
Oystercatcher, Black Turnstone and Surfbird. The rare Rock Sandpiper
is possible during winter when Sanderling are frequent. All of the regularly occurring species of alcid will be seen offshore in season including
Common Murre and Ancient Murrelet. The Ancient Murrelet are most
often seen flying past the point in small flocks far offshore. Rhinoceros
Auklet are especially numerous in summer. The rare Tufted Puffin is
seen regularly feeding with the "Rhinos"—late June through early July
is best but it will take patience and persistance to see one. Parasitic
Jaegers pass by regularly in the early morning hours, or are seen parasitizing Common Terns. When the silence is broken by screaming,
wheeling terns, one or more are in the vicinity. Long-tailed Jaeger and
Pomarine Jaeger are very rare (and often misidentified) but possible.

In summer, California and Heermann's Gulls and, during
migration and winter, Western, Mew and Thayer's Gulls rest
on the rocks. Glaucous-winged and Western x Glaucous-

winged gulls (the so-called "Puget Sound" gull) are abundant residents. To identify a "pure" Western, the head should be virtually unmarked in winter and the gull must have a yellow, not purplish-pink or pinkish-yellow, orbital ring. Check through the Bonaparte's Gulls resting on the kelp beds close to the point during July through September for a Little Gull. Once regular with one or two birds per fall in the late 1980's, this Eurasian species has become accidental once again. However, Little, Franklin's and a vagrant Black-headed Gull are possible.

One gull that has replaced the Little Gull as a regular but rare visitor to the point is the Iceland Gull. Most of the records involve first-winter birds, but adults occur. During the winter, hundreds of Thayer's Gulls feed on the offal from the sewer discharge about a mile offshore. After feeding, especially at lower tides, these gulls come to roost on the rocks around Clover Point. It is at these times that an Iceland Gull may appear and there have been one or two individuals each winter for the past five years. Most authorities consider Thayer's and Iceland Gulls to be the same species, for as they interbreed, hybrids occur and many of these individuals are found in the Victoria area.

To identify an Iceland Gull that possesses reasonably pure genes, scan the first winter Thayer's Gulls looking for one that has a mottled tail, evenly checkered tertials, a black bill with a dusky-pink base and pale primaries that have small "anchor-shaped" subapical spots. As Thayer's and Iceland Gulls are most likely the same species, their "jizz" (size, shape and proportions) are identical, although Iceland Gulls can have a smaller bill on average. The smaller barrovianus race of Glaucous Gull occurs along the west coast which should not be easily confused with Iceland Gull. Even this race can be separated by its larger "dipped in ink" bi-coloured bill and its generally heavier appearance and size. Identifying adult Iceland Gulls is very difficult. General field guides inform readers that adult Thayer's Gulls have dark eyes and that Iceland Gulls have pale primaries. In fact, 6% of Thayer's Gulls in the Victoria area have yellow eyes and a further 40-60% have gray-green eyes. Iceland Gulls can have slate-gray primaries. An adult Iceland Gull usually has less mottling on the head in winter, a smaller bill, whiter eyes and slightly paler primaries (than similarly aged Thayer's Gulls) which become "washed out" on the underwing. See Birding, October 1991, for more information as well as the gull pages at http://www.martinreid.com.

In 1983, 1992 and 1993, the warm El Nino currents brought Elegant Tern north to Canadian waters. Clover Point is one of the better sites to locate this vagrant, often found roosting on the kelp beds. Scan offshore with a scope looking for tide-lines where Red-necked Phalarope flock regularly in late summer. Numerous resident Pelagic Comorant and Double- crested Commorant fly past the point. Lately, Brandt's Cormorant have occurred in huge flocks each winter morning with smaller numbers through summer. In August and September, Bank Swallow rest with migrating swallows sunning on the hand-rails at the base of the spit on the east side. Rarely pelagics are seen from shore with records of Sabine's Gull, Northern Fulmar, Sooty Shearwater (occas-sionally numerous), Short-tailed Shearwater (rare-irregular), Fork-tailed Storm-Petrel, Leach's Storm-Petrel and Brown Pelican. Lapland Longspur, Snow Bunting and Horned Lark may be flushed from the short grass in the fall months. Harlequin Duck are resident around the shore. Many loons, grebes, and salt-water waterfowl are offshore; White-winged Scoter and Surf Scoter (common during winter) often fly past the point in summer.

Clover Point to Beacon Hill Park and Ogden Point

Back at Dallas Road, turn left (00.0 km.). Drive (0.9 km.) and turn right for Beacon Hill Park. The better birding area is at "Lovers Lane", the thickets on the right near the world's tallest totem. Many "scrub" species are present with Bushtit and Bewick's Wren. Occasionally a good drop-out of migrants may be encountered. Look for Western Wood-Pewee throughout the deciduous trees in mid-May through early June. Hermit Thrush are common migrants and often winter, feeding with Varied Thrush on fruiting shrubs along the wooded stream that connects the lakes. Victoria's only record of a Veery occurred here. There are Eurasian Wigeon among the Mallard and American Wigeon near the children's zoo. The odd American Black Duck from the introduced Yellow Point flock winters.

Continue along Dallas Road passing Douglas Street on your right. Proceed along Dallas Road (1.8 km) from Clover Point and you may turn left and park at the artificial cement pond (Dallas Road Yacht Pond). Eurasian Wigeon should be seen. One Western Gull returns to winter here annually. During the Bonaparte's Gull migration period, scope through the gulls resting on the kelp beds at the foot of Paddon Avenue where Little Gull and Franklin's Gull are possible with one record of Black-headed Gull. Bank Swallow may be encountered along the clay banks among the other migrating swallows during August and September. Scan the rocks along this coastline towards Ogden Point

Breakwall, especially Holland Point, for Wandering Tattler. Heermann's Gull are plentiful offshore.

Continue on Dallas Road for an additional (0.9 km.) (2.7 km.) and park at the Ogden Point Breakwall. The breakwall and adjacent rocks are especially good for Black Oystercatcher, Black Turnstone and Surfbird. Those seeking Black Turnstone in mid to late-July will find them here most easily. Sanderling will be seen in a small flock in winter. Brandt's Cormorant may be viewed closely off the wall in winter months. Rhinoceros Auklet are abundant in summer and a few regularly winter here. Marbled Murrelet, Common Murre and Pigeon Guillemot will be seen and occasionally Ancient Murrelet and Red Phalarope off the end of the wall in winter. The only Canadian record of Kittlitz's Murrelet was of a single bird that wintered here in 1985-86. Common Tern remain later in the year feeding along the wall into November some years. Clark's Grebe, Forster's Tern and Little Gull have been recorded and Parasitic Jaeger may be seen.

Ogden Point Breakwall to downtown Victoria

(00.0 km.) For those wishing to take the "mini-pelagic" trip on the M.V. Coho, backtrack to Oswego Street (0.1 km), turning left. You may park all day on weekends along Quebec Street without charge (0.7 km.) (0.8 km.). To reach the ticket office and to embark on the Coho, turn right at Belleville Street an additional (0.1 km.) (0.9 km.). After (0.2 km.) (1.1 km.) you will see the Blackball Ferry ticket office on your left (430 Belleville Street). (see M.V. Coho Mini-Pelagic trip p 20).

Continue driving east on Belleville Street. After (0.3 km.) (1.4 km.) you will pass the Royal British Columbia Museum on your right which is certainly worth a visit. Continuing along Belleville Street you will pass Douglas Street.

Victoria to Swan Lake Nature Sanctuary

Proceed on Belleville Street, turn left onto Blanshard Street following the Highway 17 signs and continue through downtown Victoria. After (6.0 km.) (7.4 km.) turn right off Highway 17 onto the off ramp for Highway 1 and McKenzie Avenue, turning right onto McKenzie (0.3 km.) (7.7 km.), then right onto Rainbow (0.1 km.) (7.8 km), left onto Ralph Street (0.4 km.) (8.2 km.) and then right onto Swan Lake Road to the parking lot on the left (0.1 km.) (8.3 km.).

Swan Lake Nature Sanctuary

 On the lake in the winter one should find Mute Swan, Pied-billed Grebe, Ruddy Duck, Ring-necked Duck and American Coot. Marsh Wren are resident around the lake. Many Yellow-rumped Warbler often winter in the willows. In the marshy section that lies just beyond the southern or far end ot the floating boardwalk in winter are Lincoln's Sparrow and occasionally the rare Swamp Sparrow. Virginia Rail, Yellow Warbler and Common Yellowthroat summer. An American Bittern usually winters here, seen or flushed from the cattails at the edge of the lake near the floating boardwalk.

Many swallows migrate through with the odd Tree Swallow nesting around the lake. Cooper's Hawk often hunt near the lake. The feeder behind the nature house has Spotted Towhee, Dark-eyed Junco, Fox Sparrow, Song Sparrow, White-crowned Sparrow, Golden-crowned Sparrow, with an annual White-throated Sparrow during the winter months. Walk east along the chip trail from the nature house to the bird-blind. Northern Saw-whet, Barred and Great Horned Owls have been seen roosting along the trails in the vicinity of the nature house, especially the Saw-whet during October. When a small pool or wet area remains during spring they support a few migrating shorebirds. Blue-winged Teal and Cinnamon Teal stop over in spring. The rare Swamp Sparrow has occurred at the blind in winter with up to three individuals recorded. Walk the "hedgerow" trail for migrants including Hermit Thrush. Downy Woodpecker and Bewick's Wren are common residents.

Swan Lake to Elk and Beaver Lakes

Return to Highway 17 North (Patricia Bay Highway). To do this, you must retrace your route back to Rainbow Street, then turn right at Sevenoaks Rd., then left at Neilthorpe St. to the traffic lights at McKenzie Avenue. Turn left onto McKenzie and merge right onto the highway. After driving (1.9 km) take the exit and turn right onto Quadra St. at the traffic lights (0.2 km) (2.1 km.) and immediatley left again at the next set of traffic lights onto Chatterton Way. Driving north you will pass Rithet's Bog on your right. Turn right onto Dalewood Rd. (0.8 km.) (3.0 km.) and park at its terminus (0.2 km.) (3.2 km.).

A reliable male Anna's Hummingbird can be found singing atop the hawthorn tree at the beginning of the trail. The loop around the bog is some three km in length and passes through patches of woods, willows, cattail marsh, small wet areas and brush. Cooper's Hawks nest and there are resident Virginia Rails and Ring-necked Pheasants, four pairs of Anna's and one or two Rufous Humming-birds, Marsh Wrens, Yellow Warblers, Common Yellowthroat, a pair or two of Black-headed Grosbeaks and many Red-winged Blackbirds. Lincoln's Sparrows are abundant migrants. The small remaining wet areas along Chatterton Way have wintering and migrant ducks and a few shorebirds. Swamp Sparrows have also wintered here. Rarities seen include American Avocet, Northern Mockingbird, Grasshopper Sparrow, three Bobolinks and Victoria's only record of Gray Catbird.

Retrace your route back along Chatterton Way to Quadra Street and merge onto Highway 17 North. After driving (4.4 km.) prepare to turn left for the south end of Elk lake (6.8 km.) and park your car. Elk Lake has a large raft of wintering American Coot and Common Merganser. The rare Redhead often winters with Canvasback, most recently at the small park at the north end of the lake. Pied-billed Grebe, Hooded Merganser, Gadwall and Ring-necked Duck are common in winter. Excellent trails loop the shores of both Elk and Beaver Lakes through elegant stands of Douglas-fir and tall mixed forest where an excellent array of "lowland" species will be found and possibly a Pileated Woodpecker. Circumnavigating the lake you will find Red-breasted Nuthatch, Bushtit, Chestnut-backed Chickadee, Bewick's Wren, Winter Wren, Brown Creeper, Golden-crowned Kinglet, Pine Siskin, Red Crossbill and Dark-eyed Junco throughout the year with Pacific-slope Flycatcher, Swainson's Thrush, Orange-crowned Warbler, Yellow-rumped Warbler, Townsend's Warbler, Wilson's Warbler and Cooper's Hawk in summer and Varied Thrush in winter.

(00.0 km.) Return to Highway 17 turning right. After driving (0.1 km.) turn right for Jennings Lane and park in the parking lot. In summer, Rufous Hummingbird, Yellow Warbler, Black-throated Gray Warbler and Black-headed Grosbeak (uncommon) will be found in the deciduous scrub where the lane and trail intersect. A good site for birding during migrations with warblers, sparrows and thrushes present in numbers dur-ing "drop-outs". Two species were added to the Victoria Checklist during two consecutive days in May 1986: Blackpoll Warbler and Brewer's Sparrow! A Rose-breasted Grosbeak occurred in the mid 1990's.

(00.0 km) Return to Highway 17 turning right. After (0.8 km) turn right onto Elk Lake Drive. After (0.6 km) (1.4 km.) you will pass the entrance to Beaver Lake Park. The rare Redhead is regular on the far west shoreline at the narrows where Elk and Beaver Lakes join.

Beaver Lake Park to Quick's Bottom

Continue on Elk Lake Drive. After driving (1.2 km.) (2.6 km.) turn right onto Royal Oak Drive. Alter (0.4 km.) (3.0 km.) turn right at the traffic lights onto West Saanich Road. At (0.8 km.) (3 8 km.) turn left onto Markham Road and park at the Quick's Bottom Saanich Parks and Recreation sign (0.6 km.) (4.4 km.).

Quick's Bottom

Quick's Bottom is one of the few freshwater marshes in Victoria and one of the better sites for Gadwall during the winter. Blue-winged Teal and Cinnamon Teal occur during migration. Both Sora and Virginia Rail nervously creep along the waters edge and scurry away through the thick vegetation during summer. One or two Virginia Rail winter. Marsh Wren are resident with Northern Shoveler and Lincoln's Sparrow during the winter months. Yellow Warbler and Common Yellow-throat breed and the rare Wilson's Phalarope may be regular in May. Check the northwest corner near the shed for wintering sparrows Brewer's Blackbird, Chipping Sparrow and Cliff Swallow are regular in summer.

Quick's Bottom to Viaduct, Courtland & Hastings Flats

Return to West Saanich Road and turn left for (0.6 km.), then turn left onto Beaver Lake (continue as this road changes to Beaver lake Road then Quale Road). After (1.2 km.) (1.8 km.) turn left onto Interurban Road. At (0.4 km) (2.2 km.) pull over to the left next to the metal gate, trespassing is tolerated by birders. A man-made con-struction of discarded plastic hampers, sticks and sod was built across a small creek to form the permanent wetland known as Interurban–Viaduct Flats. Unfortunately the artificial "beaver dam" destroyed the mudflats that were created each spring and fall as the flooded fields dried. This was once an important feeding site for shorebirds that require freshwater habitat. As wet fields are scarce in the Victoria region during fall migration, replacing the dam with a sluice would enable water levels to be raised and lowered to accommodate both nesting and wintering waterfowl as well as migrating shorebirds.

Wintering ducks are well represented with Northern Shoveler, Eurasian Wigeon, Ruddy Duck and by migrant Blue-winged and Cinnamon Teal. In summer the water-tolerant vegetation supports local nesting of Pied-billed Grebes, Gadwall, one or two pairs of Ring-necked Ducks and Sora. Marsh Wrens are resident and an occassional Swamp Sparrow winters.

After driving past Courtland Flats on your right (flooded in winter and good for waterfowl and shorebirds), turn right onto North Road at (2.0 km.) (4.2 km.). After (0.4 km.) (4.6 km.) turn right onto Hastings Street. At (0.8 km.) (5.4 km.) you will have reached Hastings Flats which are the southern end of Courtland Flats. Both sides of the road are productive when they are flooded in winter and early spring. Various waterfowl are found with Blue-winged Teal and Cinnamon Teal regular in migration. The flats can be excellent at times for shorebirds in spring and are the best site for Solitary Sandpiper which are found in small numbers annually. Lincoln's Sparrow and the odd Swamp Sparrow are found along the ditches in winter where Spotted Sandpiper breed in summer. Common Snipe winter in wet depressions.

Hastings Flats to Francis King Park and Munn Road

Turn left at Granville Avenue (0.1 km) (5.5 km). After (0.8 km.) (6.3 km.) turn right onto Burnside Road West. At (0.5 km.) (6.8 km.) pull into Chariton Road for Rapiers Pond on the right. Among the few shore-birds in spring, the rare Solitary Sandpiper can be seen. Blue-winged Teal, Cinnamon Teal and Common Snipe are frequently found in season. House Wren sing from the hillside.

After (0.2 km) (7.0 km.) turn right onto Prospect Lake Road. After (0.6 km.) (7.6 km.) listen for Chipping Sparrow in the garry oaks at the farm on the left. At (0.6 km.) (8.2 km.) turn left onto Munn Road. At (0.3 km.) (8.5 km.) turn right for the parking lot. Those wishing Great Horned Owl and Western Screech-Owl should continue along Prospect Lake Road to Viaduct Avenue West (approx. 2.2 km.) .

Francis King Regional Park

Francis King Park has a series of trails that wind through a sombre forest of huge Douglas-firs made more mystical by the ethereal piercing notes of the Varied Thrush. Nothing rivals the giant, ancient trees—walking among them is an experience few people will forget. Orchids and thick stands of elegant ferns decorate the moist forest floor. The song of the Winter Wren echoes in the dim and serene stillness of these deep woodlands.

Western Screech-Owl should be heard from Munn Road directly in front of the nature house so have patience and play a tape a few times. In summer a male Western Tanager sings along the road next to the nature house where Downy Woodpecker, Hairy

Woodpecker, House Wren, Pacific-slope Flycatcher, Red-breasted
Nuthatch, Warbling Vireo, Orange-crowned Warbler, Townsend's
Warbler, Chipping Sparrow and White-crowned Sparrow will be also be
found. During spring migration, a wider variety of species feed in the
broad-leaf maples and undergrowth along Munn Road.

Munn Road

Proceed along Munn Road to the trail on the left at the edge
of the powerline clearing at (0.8 km.) (9.3 km). Here, both
Hutton's Vireo and Black-throated Gray Warbler will be found.
"Squeak" often to bring the vireo into view. A walk along this trail will
be productive. Proceed along Munn Road. McGillivray's Warbler are
plentiful in the brush along the powerline clearing (0.1 km.) (9.4 km.).
Other species to be expected are California Quail, Western Screech-Owl,
Rufous Hummingbird, Willow Flycatcher, Bewick's Wren, Swainson's
Thrush, Yellow Warbler, Wilson's Warbler, Common Yellowthroat,
Spotted Towhee, Song Sparrow and White-crowned Sparrow with many
"winter" sparrows in season.

After (0.9 km) (0.2 km.) a gravel road leads into a power station.
Park at the gate and walk in. There are two small lakes that harbour
Wood Duck, Hooded Merganser, Willow Flycatcher and Yellow Warbler
in summer. House Wren and an occasional Western Tanager are behind
the station.

At (1.7 km.) (12.5 km.) check the woods on the left for Black-
throated Gray Warbler. At (0.2 km.) (12.7 km.) squeek for Hutton's Vireo
and Cassin's Vireo. After an additional (0.4 km.) (13.2km.) at the bend
in the road are Townsend's Warbler, MacGillivray's Warbler and Yellow-
rumped Warbler and at (0.7 km.) (13.9 km.) Warbling Vireo.

After (0.5 km.) (13.7 km.) you will reach a farm. Pull over on
the left. Common Snipe nest in the flooded field and may be
heard "winnowing" in twilight hours in spring and summer.
Hawk watching can be good with Bald Eagle, Sharp-shinned Hawk,
Cooper's Hawk, Red-tailed Hawk, American Kestrel and Merlin seen as
residents or during migrations. Turkey Vulture are frequent in summer.
Warbling Vireo, Cassin's Vireo, Orange-crowned Warbler and Yellow-
rumped Warbler nest along the road. Mountain Quail had their strong-
hold in the hills here years ago—"good luck".

Drive an additional (1.6 km.) (15.3 km) turning into the parking lot for

Mount Work on the right. A walk to the dry summit cloaked with arbutus will produce Blue Grouse in summer and Townsend's Solitaire in April.

At (1.8 km) (17.1 km) is a powerline clearing where Northern Pygmy-Owl are possible and Willow Flycatcher are common summer residents. Munn Road now takes a gentle turn through some beautiful moist woods at its apex and reverses on itself back towards Highway 1. As the road twists downward a fantasy land of white-barked alder forest appears, gentle and cool after the warm hillsides above. Along the drive Munn Road becomes Millstream Lake Road.

Jocelyn Hill

After driving an additional (1.1 km.) (18.2 km.) turn right off Millstream Lake Road at its junction with Millstream Road. If you proceed straight ahead, Millstream Road leads back to Highway 1 in 5.5 kilometers. Continue up Millstream Road passing Lone Tree Hill Park (2.5 km.) (20.7 km.). At (0.6 km.) (21.3 km.) Millstream Road narrows. Turn right onto Martlet Drive after (0.5 km (21.8 km.) and park at the wide area (0.4 km.) (22.2 km.) for Jocelyn Hill.

To reach the summit of Jocelyn Hill, a hike up a continuous and fairly steep grade for approximately (1.8 km.) is necessary. Proceed up Martlet Drive on foot for (0.2 km.). At 760 Martlet Drive there are two white posts, from between which is the inconspicuous trailhead. Walk over the footbridge, up the switchbacks and onto the large fallen log to the west (140 paces). From this point take the trail leading up steeply on the right. After an additional (550 paces) the damp Douglas-fir forest is replaced by a drier arbutus community with large open areas of moss-covered rocks and stunning views. It will take an additional (1200 paces) to reach the summit and an additional (450 paces) to reach the second lookout. On route to the second lookout, keep left after walking (290 paces) from the summit.

A walk up Jocelyn Hill is very unproductive during the summer months, but there are many feeding birds during late fall and early winter when the arbutus are heavily laden with fruit. The bright orange berries of the arbutus attract Hermit Thrush, American Robin, Varied Thrush, Cedar Waxwing and Purple Finch. The odd Townsend's Solitaire may be found during winter with small numbers of migrants during April. The hill has produced a few Pine Grosbeak in recent years but they are rare and not to be expected.

Jocelyn Hill—Munn / Millstream Roads to Highway 1

Return to the junction of Millstream Lake Road and Millstream Road, turning right (00.0 km.). After (5.0 km.) turn left into the Western Speedway parking lot where many Common Nighthawk are seen every summer evening. After an additional (1.6 km) (6.6 km.) or (23.7 km. from our starting point, excluding the side trip to Jocelyn Hill), you may turn right onto Highway 1 for Goldstream Park and points north (see Victoria to Goldstream Park on page XX), or left for Highway 14 and points south and west.

Highway 1 to Esquimalt Lagoon

(00.0 km.) Tum left for Highway 14. At (5.2 km.) turn right at the traffic lights onto Helmcken Road. Proceed for (1.2 km) (6.4 km.) turning right onto the Island Highway. Follow the Island Highway (Highway 14) veering left at the traffic lights at the Highway 1 junction and through Colwood. After (3.1 km.) (9.5 km.) turn left at the traffic lights onto Kuper Avenue. [It you wish, you may continue straight ahead for the Route 14 Loop (at this point named Sooke Road)]. From Kuper Avenue, turn left onto Ocean Blvd. (0.3 km.) (9.8 km.) following the signs for Fort Rodd Hill Park. After (1.0 km.) (10.8 km.) you will find Chipping Sparrow on the left. Continue past Fort Rodd Hill Park to the spit at Esquimalt Lagoon (0.5 km.) (11.3 km.).

From the corner of Highway 1 and Millstream Rd. you can also reach Esquimalt Lagoon by proceeding along Millstream Rd. over the highway and turn left onto Goldstream Ave., then left onto the Island Hwy.

Esquimalt Lagoon

The areas inside and outside the spit have a great variety of waterfowl in winter. A large raft of Western Grebe and numbers of Red-throated Loon winter offshore on the "saltchuck". Among the more common species of waterfowl wintering on the lagoon are Pied-billed Grebe, Mute Swan and Canvasback. Tufted Duck are occasionally found among the Lesser Scaup and Greater Scaup. At the entrance to the lagoon near the bridge, Brant and Caspian Tern are found in spring and many species of gull rest on the small islet including the odd Ring-billed Gull. Immature Mew Gull often summer with Western Gull expected during winter. Northern Rough-winged Swallow have nested in the neighbouring clay banks. Migrant American Pipit, Lapland

Longspur, Horned Lark and Snow Bunting are expected in the fall months, Brewer's Blackbird winter. Check the beach and inside edges for shorebirds. Wintering Black-bellied Plover, Dunlin Sanderling, migrant American Golden-Plover, Pacific Golden-Plover and resident Black Oystercatcher are among the many species of shorebird to be expected. Rarities have occured such as American Avocet, Bar-tailed Godwit, Mongolian Plover and Red-throated Pipit. Continue birding along the spit.

Esquimalt Lagoon to Witty's Lagoon

At (1.7 km) (13.0 km) turn right onto Lagoon Road. After (1.0 km) (14.0 km) turn left onto Metchosin Road and continue on Metchosin Road to Pears Road (5.4 km) (19.4 km). The entrance to Witty's Lagoon Park is to the left of Metchosin Road (0.1 km.) (19.5 km.). An alternative entrance is to turn left at Duke Road (4.1 km.) (18.1 km.), right at Cliff (0.3 km.) (18.4 km.), parking at Cliff Drive and Olympic View Road (0.4 km.) (18.8 km.). From here, take either the inconspicuous trail across the road and wade the flats, or park at the foot of Olympic View and walk the park chip trail.

Witty's Lagoon Park

From the parking lot at Witty's Lagoon you may walk down to the lagoon but keep right at the foot bridge. Various warblers and Chestnut-backed Chickadee will be encountered along the walk. The mud flats are excellent for shorebirds and gulls. Look for Semipalmated Plover, Greater Yellowlegs, Lesser Yellowlegs, Whimbrel, Semipalmated Sandpiper, Western Sandpiper, Least Sandpiper, Baird's Sandpiper, Pectoral Sandpiper, Short-billed Dowitcher, Long-billed Dowitcher and "rarities". The only record of Curlew Sandpiper for Victoria was made in 1981. Look overhead as Vaux's Swift channel through in spring and fall migration. Franklin's Gull and Little Gull have been recorded.

Witty's Lagoon to East Sooke Park

Follow Metchosin Road for an additional (1.2 km.) (20.7 km.) turning right onto Happy Valley Road, then left onto Rocky Point Road (0.7 km.) (21.4 km). After (5.4 km.) (26.8 km.) Rocky Point Road makes a sharp right as it climbs a hill and becomes East Sooke Road. [NOTE: A fair alternative site to watch for hawks and vultures, and possibly the best site for Golden Eagles, is at the corner of Rocky Point Road and Matheson Lake Park Road at (5.0 km.) (26.4 km.)]. Follow East Sooke Road through its many twists and turns for an additional (8.6 km) (35.4 km.), turning left onto Becher Bay Road to the East Sooke Park parking lot (1.8 km.) (37.2 km.).

East Sooke Park

For many years it was well-known that large "kettles" of migrant Turkey Vultures (up to a thousand individuals) passed along the Metchosin corridor in mid-September through early October, crossing the narrows of Juan de Fuca Strait at East Sooke Park where they would leave Vancouver Island. It was also known that a number of other raptor species also used this route to attempt the twenty-kilometer crossing, using the mid-day thermals. But in 1990 local birders' eyes were opened to the plethora of migrant hawks and eagles that could be seen daily!

On September 28, 1990, the first recorded Broad-winged Hawk for coastal British Columbia hightened an intense interest in the area and the subsequent observations of large movements of southbound Sharp-shinned and Red-tailed Hawks. During each of the following autumns, one or two Broad-winged Hawks have been sighted from the East Sooke lookout during their extremely small migration "window" in September. Both immature and adults birds have been recorded. Other less common species that occur in smaller numbers on good migration days (light north winds, on sunny warm days) include Osprey, Bald Eagle, Northern Harrier, Cooper's Hawk, American Kestrel, Merlin and Peregrine Falcon. Although rare, there is a fair chance of Northern Goshawk and, in early October, Rough-legged Hawk. Possibly of most interest are the numbers of Golden Eagle that pass through the region in early October (the second week of October is best), with more than a dozen birds seen on a good day.

East Sooke Park is certainly one of the best sites for viewing autumn raptor migration in the Pacific Northwest. The best time to view the spectacle is between the hours of 10:30 a.m. and 1:00 p.m.. Other local rarities such as Lewis's Woodpecker and Clark's Nutcracker have been seen at the lookout. To find the lookout for the now renowned hawk watch site, walk back to the entrance road and take the broad path (left) leading directly south from the entrance road through the cool, coastal forest. A walk to the lookout will take

20 minutes (approx. 1.5 km.) After 500 paces, proceed pass a sign for "Lookout and Coast Trail" on your left, followng the main trail signed "Cabin Point". After an additional 50 paces there is a sign for "Bamberton Hill" on the right. Stay on the main trail, go uphill, then downhill, passing another sign for "Bamberton Hill" on the right after an additional 840 paces. Still on the main trail, and still heading downhill, you will come to a fork in the main trail after another 225 paces; keep left following the sign for "Lookout"—the right trail is signed "Becher Point". After 225 paces follow the sign pointing uphill to the "Lookout". After 200 meters you will arrive at the hawk watch, overlooking the beautiful Juan de Fuca Straits and the surrounding Douglas-fir clad hills. Hawk watching can be as rewarding in the open fields adjacent to the East Sooke Park parking lot.

Durrance Lake Owling Loop

For those wishing to do some "owling", Durrance Lake Road offers a good chance to find several species. (00.0 km.). To reach Durrance Lake Road take the Royal Oak exit off the Patricia Bay Highway (Highway 17) onto Royal Oak Drive heading west. At West Saanich Road (0.7 km.) turn right (see Quick's Bottom page XX). Continue on West Saanich Road, turning left onto Wallace Drive (5.7 km) (6.4 km.), then left onto Willis Point Road (0.5 km.) (6.9 km.). Proceed along Willis Point Road for an additional (3.7 km.) (10.6 km.), turning right to Durrance Lake (0.4 km.) (11.0 km.). Western Screech-Owl, Northern Pygmy-Owl and Northern Saw-Whet Owl are often heard around the lake. Be aware, however, that while Northern Pygmy-Owl may give a long series of hoots similar to a Northern Saw-whet Owl song, the tone is different between the two species. Return to Willis Point Road and continue another (0.3 km.). Past the lake Western Screech-Owl and Northern Pygmy-Owl are often recorded.

Return to Wallace Drive, turning left (00.0 km.). After driving (1.6 km.) turn left onto Durrance Lake Road and follow it for (1.3 km.) (2.9 km.) until the road ends at a barrier. Park at the barrier and walk a short distance to the powerline clearing. A Northern Pygmy-Owl, Great Homed Owl and occasionally Western Screech-Owl may be heard. The Northern Pygmy-Owl is fairly reliable. Try for the Pygmy at twilight hours, especially just as the first rays of sunlight are visible at dawn when the owl sings for around twenty minutes. The owl is very difficult to see.

MAP 6—SOOKE

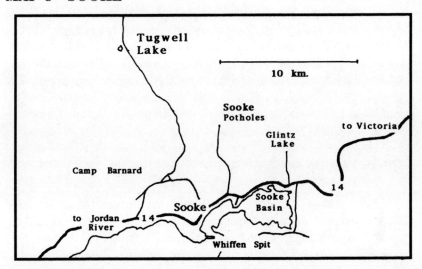

ROUTE 14 LOOP

Colwood to Glintz Lake Road

We start our trip at the corner of Highways 1 and 14 west of Victoria (see Highway 1 to Esquimalt Lagoon page 55). Turning left onto Highway 14 through Colwood, it is (37.2 km.) to downtown Sooke, a 45 minute drive.

For those who wish to try for Barred Owl, turn right off Highway 14 onto Gillespie Road just past the 17 Mile House Pub (18.7 km. from Highways 1 and14) and just before reaching Glintz Lake Road. (00.0 km). Drive for (5.7 km.) and turn right onto East Sooke Road. After driving an additional (1.9 km.) (7.6 km.) you will see the entrance to East Sooke Park. A pleasant walk for "rainforest" species. In October this is a good location to watch the Turkey Vulture "kettling". Continue an additional (2.2 km.) (9.8 km.) to the corners of Seagirt and East Sooke. Barred Owl may be lured into view in this general area by judicious use of a tape recording of their calls.

For Glintz Lake Road, turn right off Highway 14 (19.1 km) from our starting point at the corner of Highways 1 and 14.

Glintz Lake Road

A drive up this road at night or at twilight could produce Northern Pygmy-Owl, especially just before reaching the Boy Scout camp (at exactly 1.1 km.). One has been resident at this site for some time and is especially vocal between October and mid-May. This "mountain owl" is most prevalent at higher elevations. Western Screech-Owl's hollow hooting call sounds rather like a bouncing ping-pong ball and Great Horned Owl may also be heard. Dawn will find most "rain-forest" species here.

Glintz Lake Road to Sassenos

(00.0 km.) Our second stop is made at Goodridge Road in Sassenos, reached after driving an additional (13.2 km.) along Highway 14 towards Sooke. Just before turning you will pass over a small bridge. Along this creek are American Dipper in the fall and winter. Turn left onto Goodridge Road and proceed to the peninsula (0.5 km.) (13.7 km.). This general area is certainly the best area to find wintering Spotted Sandpiper on Vancouver Island. A thorough check will produce one in a mild winter. Barrow's Goldeneye are common in the area, especially behind the old mill. Use the peninsula as a vantage point for scoping Sooke Basin for waterfowl. Many Red-throated Loon, Common Murre and Marbled Murrelet are offshore. Check the log booms at the marina for wintering shorebirds—Black Turnstone, Surfbird and Black-bellied Plover. All three species of cormorant will be seen perched on log booms. A Terek Sandpiper was found here in July of 1987.

Return to Highway 14 and turn left (00.0 km.). At Sassenos access can be made to an abandoned railway track, which has now been made into a walking trail, which closely parallels Highway 14. You may turn right at either Woodland Drive or Harbour View for (0.1 km.). A walk along here offers good fall and winter birding. The following species may be found:

+	California Quail	*	Varied Thrush
+	Downy Woodpecker	+	Cedar Waxwing (R winter)
+	Northern Flicker	*	Northern Shrike R
*	Steller's Jay	+	Spotted Towhee
+	Northwestern Crow	*	Fox Sparrow
+	Chestnut-backed Chickadee	+	Song Sparrow

+ Bushtit
+ Red-breasted Nuthatch
+ Brown Creeper
+ Bewick's Wren
+ Winter Wren
* Golden-crowned Kinglet
* Ruby-crowned Kinglet
* Hermit Thrush U
+ American Robin
+ House Sparrow

* Golden-crowned Sparrow
+ White-crowned Sparrow (UW)
* Dark-eyed Junco
+ Purple Finch
+ House Finch
+ Red Crossbill (erratic)
+ Pine Siskin
+ American Goldfinch (R W)
* Evening Grosbeak

SUMMER:

Rufous Hummingbird
Pacific-slope Flycatcher
Swainson's Thrush
Warbling Vireo

Orange-crowned Warbler
MacGillivray's Warbler
Wilson's Warbler

KEY TO SYMBOLS

* winter (W)   + all year   R-rare   U-uncommon

Sooke River Estuary and Billings Spit

After an additional (2.0 km.) turn left at the gravel pit onto Idlemore Road. After (0.8 km.) (2.8 km.) turn right onto Kaltasin Road for (0.1 km.) (2.9 km) and then straight through on the dirt trail under the trees at the comer of Billings Road. Beyond lies the Sooke River Estuary, an important wintering area for waterfowl and migrating shorebirds. Most species of dabbling ducks are represented including Green-winged Teal, Mallard, Northern Pintail, Northern Shoveler (rare), Gadwall, Eurasian Wigeon (very good site), American Wigeon, Canvasback (uncommon), Greater Scaup, Lesser Scaup (uncommon), Hooded Merganser and Common Merganser. Most sea ducks will be found in other areas of the basin with Oldsquaw, Black Scoter (a small number annually), Surf Scoter, White-winged Scoter, Common Goldeneye, Barrow's Goldeneye, Bufflehead and Red-breasted

Merganser. All three common loon species are represented with the odd Yellow-billed Loon seen on rare occasions. All grebes are found here with the odd Pied-billed Grebe and Eared Grebe. A few pairs of Mute Swan inhabit the basin. Check the gulls in winter for Mew Gull, Thayer's Gull, Glaucous-winged Gull, with the occasional Western Gull, Herring Gull and Glaucous Gull (rare). An old record of King Eider and a recent record of Emperor Goose show the possibilities of finding rare waterfowl.

This is the only regular site for Ruddy Turnstone during spring migration along the east coast of Vancouver Island. Although found from late April they are best looked for from May 5-15. Semipalmated Plover and hundreds of Black Turnstone use this estuary as a spring stopover in early May. Fall migration brings the usual southern Vancouver Island species. This is one of the better sites, along with Esquimalt Lagoon, for finding Caspian Terns. This large tern does not breed on the island and usually arrives in early May and departs in early August. It can be found resting on the mudflats here particularly from mid-May to early June. A low or flooding tide is best for locating them.

A drive or walk to the foot of Billings Road (0.1 km) will give access to scoping other areas of the basin and Billings Spit. Check any feeders in the area in winter (a Brambling was found here in November 1983). A walk along the beach may produce a Spotted Sandpiper at any time of the year. The brushy neighbourhood produces perfect habitat to delay warblers in the late fall and early winter. Sooke and Sassenos are particularly reliable for finding Evening Grosbeak feeding in the maples especially during winter. Red-breasted Sapsuckers are also fairly reliable in the fruit trees and cedars during winter.

Sooke River Estuary to Sooke

(00.0 km) Return to Highway 14 and turn left towards Sooke. After driving (1.3 km) you will see Sooke River Road on the night. If you wish to see American Dipper, drive five kilometers to the Sooke Potholes where they are resident. In the summer months the dippers retreat a short way upstream. Continue to downtown Sooke and Otterpoint Road (1.6 km.) (2.9 km).

Sooke River to Tugwell Lake

 Sooke lies in the extreme southwest parameter of the Southeast Coastal Lowlands. Leaving Sooke for Tugwell Lake you will be venturing into the East Coast bio-geoclimatic zone, leaving Southeast Coastal Lowland species below at lower elevations. When travelling to Tugwell Lake be sure to check your spare tire and gas up. Roads are gravel but are in good shape, although travel is only allowed on weekends. Traffic is moderate, so if help is needed you should not feel isolated. (00 0 km.). Turn right at the lights in the center of Sooke onto Otterpoint Road north and west for (4.8 km) to Young Lake Road.

Black-throated Gray Warbler are to be found in the mixed deciduous areas along the length of Otterpoint Road, as well as other common species found in this habitat. Turn right (north) along Young Lake Road for (0.4 km.) (5.2 km.). In the stand of second-growth Douglas-firs is a small breeding colony of Hammond's Flycatcher. Proceed (0.1 km.) (5.3 km.) and turn right at Camp Barnard. You are now on Butler Main logging road. (If you wish, drive into the camp property. After asking permission, check the trees around the camp buildings for Red-breasted Sapsucker). Stay on Butler Main watching for the km. markers along the roadside. Between kilometer marker nine and ten (11.7 km) (17.0 km.) is an access road on the left closed by a yellow metal gate. Here, at 2,500-3,000 feet you have entered the East Coast bio-geoclimatic zone.

Tugwell Lake

The "specialities" for Tugwell Lake include Blue Grouse, Ruffed Grouse, Red-breasted Sapsucker and Gray Jay. Yellow-rumped Warbler (Audubon's) are common summer residents. The Gray Jay is found uncommonly on walks in this area, but extensive driving, especially during the fall and winter, will enable the birder to locate a small group. Blue Grouse will be heard booming everywhere immediately after leaving the car (April to September). Ruffed Grouse should be heard drumming in willowy and alder areas in spring or flushed along the numerous trails. Red-breasted Sapsuckers' Morse code drumming should be heard April to June. They may be difficult to find (uncommon) due to their secretive nature. Look and listen between km. markers 7.5 and 10.5. In the many dead standing trees riddled with nesting holes one may find the rare Western Bluebird, and, if very fortunate, a Northern Pygmy-Owl may call during the day. Hairy Woodpecker are the dominate Picoides woodpecker in the area.

Finding Tugwell Lake itself is rather difficult. Walk through the yellow gate following the main track—keeping left and ignoring branch trails— until you reach the main river crossing of Tugwell Creek (approximately

1.5 km.). Here you will find Willow Flycatcher. Then retrace your steps back to the first trails on your right. The lake is 0.5 km. away. To reach Butler Main, continue past the lake on a very steep and rough wash-out to the road (0.5 km.). You should then walk to the left to your vehicle.

Other passerines occuring here in summer include: Common Nighthawk, Rufous Hummingbird, Olive-sided Flycatcher, Pacific-slope Flycatcher, Willow Flycatcher (rare-local), Spotted Towhee (uncommon), Townsend's Solitaire (rare), Swainson's Thrush, American Robin, Cassin's Vireo, Hutton's Vireo (rare), Warbling Vireo, Orange-crowned Warbler, Yellow Warbler, Yellow-rumped Warbler, Common Yellowthroat, Townsend's Warbler and MacGillivray's Warbler. Wilson's Warbler are found more commonly at lower elevations along Butler Main and Otterpoint Roads. Residents include: Steller's Jay, Chestnut-backed Chickadee, Red-breasted Nuthatch (uncommon), Winter Wren, Golden-crowned Kinglet, Varied Thrush, Song Sparrow, Dark-eyed Junco, Purple Finch, Pine Siskin and Red Crossbill.

Ruby-crowned Kinglet is mainly a migrant (vagrant in summer). The bog near the gate has Common Yellowthroat and nesting Hooded Merganser. Occasionally one will find Yellow Warbler and Willow Flycatcher. A singing male Magnolia Warbler was found here in June 1983 and a nesting pair of Red-breasted x Red-naped Sapsuckers that raised hybrid young. Proof that rare birds may be found in the most unlikely places.

Hermit Thrush and Fox Sparrow, two species as yet unrecorded as breeding species within the Victoria checklist area, most likely nest on the Weeks Lake Plateau. Although the plateau has been surveyed, a breeding individual might be located by someone with initiative. This region lies on the extreme western edge of the checklist area and is a further fifteen kilometers up Butler Main and approximately 750 feet higher in elevation. Hermit Thrushes have been recorded in summer at Mount Brenton in the East Coast zone west of Chemainus, just three or four kilometers west of the Victoria checklist area boundry. Gray Jays and Northern Pygmy-Owls are also frequently found here.

Tugwell Lake or Sooke to Whiffen Spit

Our last stop is just beyond Sooke Return to downtown Sooke, turning right at the stoplights, and continue west on Highway 14 (00.0 km.). Drive for (1.7 km.) to Whiffen Spit Road, turn left and continue to its end an additional (1.5 km) (3.2 km.). Park your car and walk up the spit.

Whiffen Spit

The spit is good for scoping yet another area of Sooke Basin and the outer ocean. Most Common Tern reach their westerly limits here (some to Orveas Bay). Check through the gulls as Westerns are prevalent here, especially in August. The more common alcids will be found offshore. Shorebirding can be fair here with the uncommon American Golden-Plover and Pacific Golden-Plover most years. Black Oystercatcher are to be found regularly.

Snow Bunting and Lapland Longspur are regular (both uncommon) in the fall months. A wagtail species was seen here in May 1980 and a Gray-crowned Rosy Finch in the mid 1990's.

Whiffen Spit to Point-No-Point

Continue from the corners of Whiffen Spit and Highway 14 turning left towards Jordan River. Be sure to "gas up" for the next leg as there are no gas stations at Jordan River.

After driving (48.8 km) from our starting point at Highways 1 & 14 you will reach French Beach Provincial Park. Birding is poor in the older second-growth forest. Hutton's Vireo are easy to find around the parking lot and the odd Red-breasted Sapsucker may be encountered in cold weather. Continue west on Highway 14 through a tunnel of moss-draped trees.

Point-No-Point

About twenty-four kilometers from Sooke, or (52.0 km) from our starting point at the corner of Highways 1 & 14] you will find the Point-No-Point Resort. There are some pleasant trails and scenic views but ask permission to use the trails. Birding is poor on land but offshore Red Phalarope and Black-legged Kittiwake are possible in the fall.

Point-No-Point to Jordan River

Continue west on Highway 14 an additional (8 0 km.) to Jordan River. You will find the weather much cooler here than at Victoria in any season.

To reach Jordan River from the Victoria area take a pleasant, scenic 60 kilometer drive from the corner of Highways 1 & 14. Turn onto Highway 14 driving through Colwood and continue (26 km.) to Sooke. Drive west past Sooke (32 km.) along paved coastal

Highway 14 to Port Renfrew. For those wishing to drive straight through it is a one-hour drive.

Jordan River

The actual division between the East and West Coast bio-geoclimatic zones on Southern Vancouver Island is just east of Jordan River. For ease of recognition Jordan River is considered the border, where the status of birds is "West Coast". As Jordan River is where "east meets west" some overlap occurs with such eastern species as Turkey Vulture, California Quail, Violet-green Swallow, Barn Swallow, Western Wood-Pewee, Willow Flycatcher, Bushtit, Bewick's Wren, Western Tanager and Lincoln's Sparrow.

In the slash just before entering Jordan River look for California Quail, MacGillivray's Warbler, Willow Flycatcher, Common Nighthawk (evenings), Bewick's Wren, Pileated Woodpecker (one resident pair), Turkey Vulture (rare), American Goldfinch, and many sparrows including Golden-crowned Sparrow. Lincoln's Sparrow are abundant in autumn.

MAP 7—ROUTE 14 / MAP 8—JORDAN RIVER

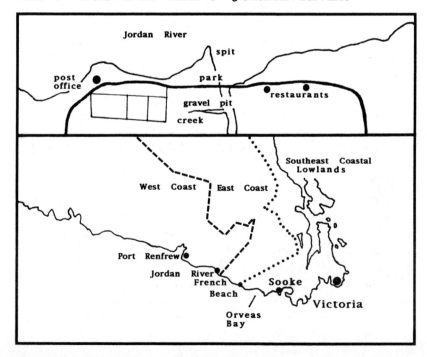

Many Victoria birders come to add Black-legged Kittiwake to their year-lists. These are found from October to early December just off the mouth of the river in the tide-rip after strong westerly winds. The best time to look for this pelagic gull is around noon when they come in to bathe. They are seen on the horizon line regularly. Herring Gull (winter) and Western Gull (especially in August) are fairly common on the spit at the mouth of the river, uncommon at Victoria. Red-throated Loon are common offshore in winter and, typical of the west coast, also seen occasionally in summer.

After checking offshore, walk through the gravel pit following the creek eastwards. At the corner of the gravel pit and the logging community are blackberry thickets where wintering flocks of sparrows contain White-crowned Sparrow, Golden-crowned Sparrow, Fox Sparrow and Song Sparrow. Walk along the many back roads in town. A Bewick's Wren is usually near the tennis court (November-December). Fox Sparrow (fuliginosa) are a common breeding species in the brush, especially near the hill by the post office. Their breeding corresponds exactly with west coast habitat—they are residents here.

Walk back to your car via the offices and follow the shoreline checking for vagrants and rare west coast species. This area seems to be a trap for rarities with records of Eastern, Western and Tropical Kingbirds, a juvenile wagtail species (White or Black-backed), Northern Mockingbird, Palm and Canada Warblers, Grasshopper and Swamp Sparrows and Rustic Bunting. Less rare are records of Yellow-billed Loon and White-throated Sparrows. Shorebirds and puddle birds are poorly represented here, although Red Phalarope is regular in late fall. Numbers of Brown Pelicans have increased during the fall months on Southern Vancouver Island and Jordan River has become one of the most reliable places to see this bird in Canada.

Just past the Breakers Restaurant, Highway 14 takes a sharp right. A gravel road is found here that parallels the back of the log dump and terminates at the power station. A locked gate may be passed on foot. Species that are frequently found on a walk here include Hairy Woodpecker, Downy Woodpecker, Pacific-slope Flycatcher, Warbling Vireo and many migrants in season. Hutton's Vireo are constantly heard singing their monotonous "zeer zeer zeer" or "zu-weep zu-weep zu-weep" from the damp, mixed forests containing cedar, alder, and Douglas-fir. Hutton's Vireo do not inhabit oak forests in British Columbia as they do in the southern sector of their U.S.A. range.

Proceed up the highway to the top of the hill (0.5 km.). The highway makes a sharp left turn. At this corner a pair of Western Screech-Owl can be enticed to taped calls and seen easily by flashlight. Ignore the "main" logging road that branches off Highway 14 and walk or drive the trail that goes to the right, then immediately left. After a short distance you will see a drop-off with the power station below. Townsend's Warbler and Hutton's Vireo are found at this corner. Proceed along the road until you see a large pipe that feeds water to the power station. Look overhead for both Black Swift and Vaux's Swift in season. Jordan River may be the most consistent area to see swifts in migration on Vancouver Island. Thousands of Vaux's Swift pass through annually in early September. The very deep "booming" of the Blue Grouse will be "felt" more than heard.

 The following is a general list of abundant—uncommon species to be expected at Jordan River For further information use Column 2 on the Checklist:

Red-throated Loon
Pacific Loon
Common Loon
Horned Grebe
Red-necked Grebe
Western Grebe
Double-crested Cormorant
Brandt's Cormorant
Pelagic Cormorant
Great Blue Heron
Canada Goose
Brant
Mallard
Northern Pintail
American Wigeon
Green-winged Teal
Greater Scaup
Oldsquaw
White-winged Scoter
Surf Scoter
Common Goldeneye
Bufflehead
Hooded Merganser
Common Merganser

Belted Kingfisher
Red-breasted Sapsucker (R)
Hairy Woodpecker
Downy Woodpecker
Northern Flicker
Olive-sided Flycatcher
Pacific-slope Flycatcher
Violet-green Swallow
Northern Rough-winged Swallow
Barn Swallow
Steller's Jay
Northwestern Crow
Common Raven
Chestnut-backed Chickadee
Red-breasted Nuthatch (R)
Winter Wren
Golden-crowned Kinglet
Ruby-crowned Kinglet
Swainson's Thrush
Hermit Thrush
American Robin
Varied Thrush
Cedar Waxwing
American Pipit

Red-breasted Merganser
Bald Eagle
Sharp-shinned Hawk
Red-tailed Hawk
Peregrine Falcon
Blue Grouse
Ruffed Grouse
Bonaparte's Gull
Mew Gull
California Gull
Heermann's Gull
Thayer's Gull
Common Murre
Pigeon Guillemot
Marbled Murrelet
Ancient Murrelet
Rhinoceros Auklet
Band-tailed Pigeon
Northern Pygmy-Owl
Western Screech-Owl
Vaux's Swift
Black Swift
Rufous Hummingbird

European Starling
Hutton's Vireo
Warbling Vireo
Orange-crowned Warbler
Yellow Warbler
Yellow-rumped Warbler
Townsend's Warbler
Common Yellowthroat
MacGillivray's Warbler
Wilson's Warbler
Savannah Sparrow
Fox Sparrow
Song Sparrow
Golden-crowned Spanrow
White-crowned Sparrow
Dark-eyed Junco
Spotted Towhee
Brown-headed Cowbird
Purple Finch
Red Crossbill
Pine Siskin
American Goldfinch

Jordon River to Port Renfrew

Continue west on Highway 14 towards Port Renfrew (00.0 km). Starting from the drive-in restaurant in Jordan River you will see North Main Logging Road on your right at (2.7 km.). North Main is only open to private vehicles on weekends! Veer to the left (1.7 km.) (4.4 km.) after leaving Highway 14. Gray Jay may be located at Wye Creek around the six kilometer marker (yellow topped poles). Other species in the vicinity include Hairy Woodpecker, Varied Thrush, Hermit Thrush and Pacific-slope Flycatcher. Blue Grouse are often common in the logging slashes along the drive.

Return to Highway 14 and turn right towards Port Renfrew (00.0 km.). Soon you will pass China Beach Park where the birding is poor, then Loss Creek Park (17.0 km.) (neither park has camping facilities). At (36.0 km.) you will be in the vicinity of a Vaux's Swift colony. Scan the open sky above you in summer for the bat-like flight of this cigar-shaped aerial feeder.

Port Renfrew

At (39.3 km.) (101.0 km. from Victora) turn right on Deering Road. After an additional (0.5 km.) (39.8 km.) turn left onto the sand-spit. Here in winter you may scope the Port of San Juan and the cove. The usual west coast loons, grebes, ducks and cormorants will be encountered: Common Loon, Red-throated Loon, Horned Grebe, Red-necked Grebe, Western Grebe, Bufflehead, Greater Scaup, White-winged Scoter, Surf Scoter, Oldsquaw and Marbled Murrelet. Black Turnstone and various gulls will be seen on the spit.

MAP 9 PORT RENFREW

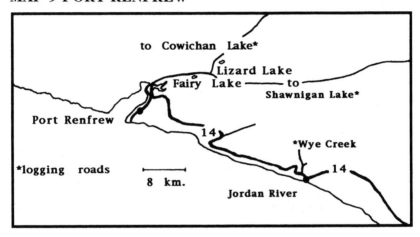

Back on Deering Road, turn left, then right onto Island Road an additional (0.5 km) (40.3 km.). This drive will take you through riverine byways of the estuary where Hooded Merganser and Pied-billed Grebe (rare) should be found. Make a "U" turn at the farm-yard (1.9 km.) (42.2 km.) and return to Deering Road checking for shorebirds during migration months. Turn right onto Deering Road (00.0 km.). At the fork (0.3 km.) keep to the right. Just after crossing the bridge (1.5 km.) (1.8 km.) keep to the right for Fairy Lake at the sign for Lake Cowichan, or left for the R.V park or the marina.

On the way to Fairy Lake check the marshy area along the road (0.6—1.1 km) (2.4—2.9 km.) for Marsh Wren in winter. At the Fairy Lake campsite sign, turn right (0.2 km.) (3.1 km.). Here in the mixed habitat around the lake you will find many of the common west coast species listed under Jordan River with Pied-billed Grebe, Red-throated Loon, Hooded Merganser and Common Goldeneye on the lake.

Lizard Lake is nearby (8.1 km) (11.2 km.). Turn right after leaving Fairy Lake. The road to Lizard Lake is paved with broken stretches. After driving (6.4 km) from Fairy Lake take the left-hand fork (the right-hand goes to Shawnigan Lake which is approximately 50 km. away). Here at Lizard Lake, at a slightly higher elevation, you will find most of the "rainforest" species including Varied Thrush, Chestnut-backed Chickadee and Golden-crowned Kinglet. Pavement ends soon after. You may continue through to Lake Cowichan approximately 42 km.—32 km. of which are on logging road.

Retrace your route back to the bridge at the junction to Port Renfrew and the marina and R.V. park (00.0 km). After turning left over the bridge, turn right at the fork (0.1 km.). After (0.9 km) (1.0 km) Trumpeter Swan will be found in the estuary during winter. Continue back towards Port Renfrew—at the corner of Highway 14 (Parkinson Road) and Deering Road, turn right for Port Renfrew. After (0.2 km.) (1.2 km) there is a gas station. After an additional (0.2 km) (1.4 km.) you may turn left for Botanical Beach for some tide-pool exploration. Cerantes Road is four kilometers of very rough road to the pools. An additional (0.4 km) (1.8 km) drive will bring you to the end of the government wharf. The rare Yellow-billed Loon has been seen on occasion. A restaurant and pub are located at the end of the pier.

Map 10—MALAHAT—DUNCAN LOOP

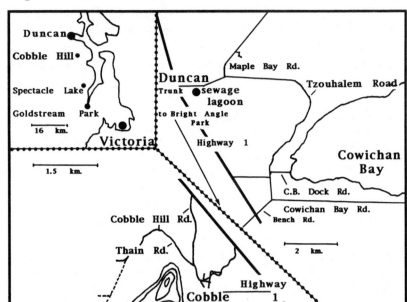

MALAHAT—DUNCAN LOOP

This entire trip lies within the boundaries of the Southeast Coastal Lowlands on Southern Vancouver Island.

The Cowichan Estuary is more deciduous than the Saanich Peninsula and Red-eyed Vireo are fairly common and widespread in the cotton-woods along the numerous waterways. Black-headed Grosbeak are wide-spread in the numerous damp, osier scrub thickets. Black-throated Gray Warbler are also numerous in the available second-growth deciduous areas. More wet areas are found here, supporting nesting dabbling ducks, mergansers, Common Snipe (Somenos—Quamichan Lakes) and other marsh species.

The specialities to search for are American Dipper (Goldstream Provincial Park), Hammond's Flycatcher (Spectacle Lake Park), Green Heron, Black Swift, Ring-billed Gull and Purple Martin (Cowichan Bay), and Wood Duck (Duncan Sewage Lagoons).

Victoria to Goldstream Provincial Park

Start your trip at Highway 1 (Douglas Street) in Victoria at the Town and Country Shopping Plaza (see Saanich Peninsula map on page 25), driving west towards Duncan (00.0 km.). After driving (15.8 km.) you will enter Goldstream Provincial Park. Turn right at the visitor area and park.

Goldstream Provincial Park

In the narrow Goldstream gorge rainfall is not persistant but rainforest conditions exist because it is so sheltered from sun and wind that water evaporates slowly. As a result there are big trees, mossy boughs, and dense undergrowth like that of a true rainforest. In and around the small rapids along the Goldstream River, which runs through the park alongside the highway, the American Dipper will be found all year. In summer check under the bridges as the American Dipper frequently nests beneath them. Resident Varied Thrush and Hairy Woodpecker may be found along the many trails. The Varied Thrush find suitable nesting in the damp forest on the higher trails and a pair or two may remain all summer long. The song of mournful quality drifts down the inclines to the valley all through the breeding season.

During the salmon spawning season in late fall many species of gull come to feed, among them one or two Glaucous Gulls. Barrow's Goldeneye frequent the river mouth in winter. Red-breasted Sapsucker may be seen in cedars around the main picnic table area during the winter months. Hermit Thrush too are prevalent during winter. A Northern Pygmy-Owl is frequently heard around the amphitheatre which is located at the Goldstream Provincial Park campsite to the southwest of Highway 1 (look for signs coming from Victoria).

Goldstream Park to Spectacle Lake

Return to the highway and turn right—driving along the Malahat Drive. The view of the Saanich Peninsula and the Gulf Islands from an elevation of 1,000 feet is breathtaking. At the summit of the Malahat turn left onto Whittaker Road at the sign for Spectacle Lake Park (10.6 km) (26.4 km).

Spectacle Lake Park

Just after leaving the highway there is a stand of second-growth Dougas-fir where Hammond's Flycatcher are common from late April to September. After singing stops in July they are more difficult to find. The song consists of three parts, all "burry". This species is found in scattered small numbers on the Saanich Peninsula but is found more readily from the Malahat northward along the Island's east coast. Townsend's Warbler is abundant in the same small firs along with the "Audubon's" Yellow-rumped Warbler. MacGillivray's Warbler sings all summer long from the thickets of salal and surrounding underbrush. Alders along the road harbour Warbling Vireo.

Continue driving along the road to the powerline clearing. Steller's Jay can be found here in summer (uncommon resident) after they have left their wintering grounds at lower elevations on the Saanich Peninsula. The very rare Mountain Quail was last confirmed in this area in August 1986 so be alert to any quail observed. However, it is most likely that the original stock has been extirpated. Turkey Vulture often float by on still wings overhead. Olive-sided Flycatchers' "drink three-beers" are emitted from distant snags and the "croak" of the Common Raven is uttered persistently. In the more open areas jewel-like Rufous Hummingbird dart about abundantly and the beautifully decorated White-crowned Sparrow breed.

Continue down the road to the park. Hammond's Flycatcher should be found around the lake and fortunate observers may find resident Red-breasted Sapsucker in the alders. A hike into the hills should produce Blue Grouse and Ruffed Grouse. In the conifer sections Steller's Jay, Red Crossbill and Pine Siskin are resident.

Spectacle Lake to Mill Bay and Cobble Hill

Returning to the highway, turn left towards Duncan (00.0 km.). After (11.0 km.) you will pass through the town of Mill Bay. Turn right and check the bay for the rare Yellow-billed Loon, a regular location for migrants during late winter. Returning to the highway, turn right towards Duncan and drive to the traffic lights at the corner of Highway 1 and Cobble Hill Road (19.3 km. from Spectacle Lake). Turn left onto Cobble Hill Road towards Cobble Hill. Drive (1.8 km) (21.1 km.) and turn right onto Thain Road, then drive an additional (1.4 km) (22.5 km.) and stop at an unnamed gravel road.

Cobble Hill and Old Bamberton Quarry

A pair of Black-throated Gray Warbler nest at the corner of the gravel road and Thain Road. Along Thain Road, Pacific-slope Flycatcher, Chestnut-backed Chickadee, Warbling Vireo, Cassin's Vireo, Hutton's Vireo, Orange-crowned Warbler, Wilson's Warbler, Townsend's Warbler and MacGillivray's Warbler will be encountered during the breeding season.

Continue along Thain Road for an additional (0.9 km.) (23.4 km.) where the road changes to gravel. After another (1.2 km.) (24.6 km.) (a total of 3.8 km. from Cobble Hill Road) turn right down a short dirt road and park. The ploughed fields in front of you are known as Cobble Meadows. A small population of Vesper Sparrow bred in the surrounding upland pastures in the past but the sneezy "fitz-bew" of the Willow Flycatcher will still be heard from the thickets This is private property so be respectful!

Continue on Thain Road for an additional (0.6 km) (25.2 km) and park at the powerline clearing and walk right (west). A hike along the numerous old roads and trails at the Old Bamberton Quarry will produce such common breeding species as Spotted Sandpiper, California Quail, House Wren, Northern Rough-winged Swallow and Willow Flycatcher.

Cobble Hill to Cowichan Bay

Retrace your route to Highway 1 and turn left towards Duncan (00.0 km). If you wish to try for Barred Owl, turn left just past the Payless gas station onto Koksilah Road at the sign for Bright Angel Park (4.3 km.). Proceed along Koksilah Road passing Bench Road to Tigwell Road (3.1 km.) (7.4 km.), turning right to the park entrance road (0.5 km.) (7.9 km) along which the the owls are heard. A walk along one of the many trails through this cedar-filled bottomland will produce the usual "rainforest" species including Hutton's Vireo.

(00.0 km.) Retrace your route to Bench Road (1.1 km.) and turn left, pass over Highway 1 at the gas station (1.7 km.) (2.8 km.) or (5.2 km. from Cobble Hill Road) or (50.9 km. from Victoria—a 45 minute drive) and proceed along Bench Road. Drive (0.8 km.) (3.6 km.) to Cowichan Bay Road, turn left onto Cowichan Bay Road and continue for an additional (0.9 km.) (4.5 km.)

Cowichan Bay

Turn right at the large sign Cowichan Bay Dock Road, also known as the CNR Dock Road looking carefully at the edges of the waterways for Green Heron hidden in the brushy margins. These secretive herons are uncommon from mid-April through August.

After driving an additional (0.7 km) (5.2 km) you will see a wet field on the right. This area has produced many rarities including Great Egret, Snowy Egret and Ruff. Many species of shorebirds are well represented here including both species of dowitcher (the Long-billed Dowitcher is the more common of the two here) and American Golden-Plover and Pacific Golden-Plover (uncommon in the fall). Small numbers of Semipalmated Sandpiper are regularly found among the many Western Sandpiper and Least Sandpiper. The rare Wilson's Phalarope has nested here. Occasionally Blue-winged Teal, Cinnamon Teal, Northern Shoveler, American Wigeon and Gadwall have remained in summer to nest. Cowichan Bay is the best site on Vancouver Island to search among the many Pectoral Sandpiper in the fall for the very rare Sharp-tailed Sandpiper. Virtually all of the rarer shorebirds could show and Stilt Sandpiper occurs.

The brushy margins along the road are good for finding various sparrows, warblers and Rufous Hummingbird. This is a good area for finding vagrants such as kingbirds, Palm Warbler and Yellow-headed Blackbird. Short-eared Owl are occasionally flushed from the grassy road margins or adjacent marshy areas during fall migration or during winter. Watch for Black Swift (early June) and Vaux's Swift high overhead. Bank Swallow could be seen during fall migration. Bushtit, Bewick's Wren, American Pipit, Cedar Waxwing, Northern Shrike, Purple Finch and House Finch are seen in season. Peregrine Falcon are known to nest on the high, rock bluffs of Mount Tzouhalem which form a dramatic backdrop to "The Bay". Often, the Peregrines are seen feeding across the flats throughout the year. Northern Harrier, Merlin, and other raptors are possible.

Continue to drive or walk for another (0.6 km.) (5.8 km.). On the left, Cowichan Bay supports many resident feral Mute Swan. Gulls are often numerous with Glaucous Gull recorded annually during winter and Ring-billed Gull from late June to early November while rare individuals winter. This is the best area for seeing Ring-billed Gull on eastern Vancouver Island (up to 60 daily); they are relatively uncommon elsewhere on the east coast. Look for the Purple Martin nest boxes on the pilings on the right (south) side of the road. The pilings project from the mudflats at low tide or sit out in the bay at higher tides. This is the most convenient and reliable site on southern Vancouver Island to see Purple Martin usually from mid-April to late August. The nest boxes on the left are full of Tree Swallow. An Osprey nest will be seen atop a man-made structure on the left (north) at the edge of the lumber yard. Check for numerous waterfowl in winter on the bay including Barrow's Goldeneye amongst the logs. Tufted Duck has been recorded with the Greater Scaup. An occasional Caspian Tern may be seen in summer usually May to July flying over the bay. Sandhill Crane are rare but regular migrants in mid-September in the grassy fields surrounding the estuary.

Retrace your route to the CNR Dock Road sign. Walk over the bridge on Tzouhalem Road to the right and walk along the gravel dike road. Immediately on the left Red-eyed Vireo will be found in the cottonwoods. An occasional Black-headed Grosbeak may be in the area. Green Heron have been seen in the past along the creek partially concealed by brush where the dike road turns sharply to the right and swings around close to the main river. Walk back to your car.

(00.0 km) The Cowichan Bay Road has now changed name to Tzouhalem Road. Turn right off the CNR Dock Road onto Tzouhalem Road. Stop after driving (0.5 km.) at the second bridge and check for Green Heron then proceed for (0.9 km.) (1.4 km) to the fourth bridge. A walk on the dike road to the left will produce Red-eyed Vireo and Black-headed Grosbeak and yet another chance for Green Heron. A walk along the Doman Dike to the right passing over three fences by way of ladder-bridges will take you past small marshes that harbour Marsh Wren to salt marshes at the head of Cowichan Bay. Northern Harrier are often seen hunting over the area. A recent record of Black-crowned Night-Heron was made here and a Cattle Egret was recorded during a past winter at the farm on Tzouhalem Road.

Cowichan Bay to Mount Tzouhalem

Continue along Tzouhalem Road for (3.1 km) (4.5 km.) to the junction of Tzouhalem and Maple Bay Roads and turn right on Maple Bay Road (00.0 km). Drive for (2.9 km.) turning right onto Kingsview Road at the properties sign. Continue for (0.8 km.) (3.7 km.) then turn right onto Belcarra Road for another (0.8 km.) (4.5 km.) and then left onto Chippawa for (0.3 km.) (4.8 km). Park at the end of Chippawa.

Mount Tzouhalem

From this point walk along the wide jeep trail for 400 paces until you see the ecological reserve sign on your right. A few more yards on the narrow trail will bring you to a steel fence. The ecological reserve of Mount Tzouhalem lies beyond. Occasionally Townsend's Solitaire are found during their April migration period. This is an interesting area to visit and the view is magnificent.

Mount Tzouhalem to Quamichan Lake

Retrace your route to the junction of Maple Bay and Tzouhalem Roads and en route you will pass Indian Road on the right (0.1 km.) before the junction. A drive to the foot of Indian Road (0.7 km.) will bring you to a small park at Quamichan Lake.

Quamichan Lake

Quamichan Lake harbours the greatest diversity of freshwater waterfowl in the Duncan region during the winter. Scope for Bald Eagle, Double-crested Cormorant, Great Blue Heron, Mute Swan, Canada Goose, American Black Duck (rare), Mallard, American Wigeon, Canvasback, Ring-necked Duck, Lesser Scaup, Common Goldeneye (scarce), Barrow's Goldeneye, Bufflehead and Hooded Merganser. Hundreds of Common Merganser and American Coot will be seen. A large raft of Ruddy Duck winter at the foot of Moose Road off Lakes Road to the west and may be seen with a scope from this vantage point. An excellent assortment of gulls come to be hand-fed. In winter, among the common Glaucous-winged Gull and Thayer's Gull, you may find the odd rarity such as Ring-billed Gull, California Gull and Western Gull.

Cowichan Lake to Duncan Sewage Lagoons

Return to the junction, turning right onto Tzouhalem Road towards Duncan (00.0 km.). After driving (0.6 km.) you will cross over a small bridge. Turn left on the dirt road. This is the entrance to the Duncan Sewage Lagoons.

Duncan Sewage Lagoons

Check the creeks that flow around the perimiter for Green Heron. Possibly the best site on the Island for this secretive heron is to walk the dike at the southwest corner which leads to the Cowichan River and fish hatchery. Yellow Warbler, Willow Flycatcher and Black-headed Grosbeak will be heard in the willows here. As parking may be a problem you should drive to the opposite side of the lagoons (00.0 km.). Continue driving along Tzouhalem which becomes Trunk Road at Lakes Road (on the right) en route (0.3 km.) and turn left at Marchmount Road (0.9 km.) (1.2 km) to its end and park (0.8 km) (2.0 km.). To reach the sewage lagoons from downtown Duncan, turn right at the traffic lights at Trunk Road and drive straight onto Marchmount Road to its end (1.5 km.). There are "postings" but birders are tolerated.

The aesthetics are not pleasant but the ponds are good for ducks, especially Wood Duck which are common in summer and scarce in winter. Tufted Duck have been recorded several times in February among the hundreds of Lesser Scaup. Blue-winged Teal and Cinnamon Teal are regular during migration and in late summer. Various gulls are recorded in season. Bonaparte's Gull commonly perch on the power lines from July through November. The fairly rare Franklin's Gull is annual, usually in September or October, but into December some years with eight recorded in 1987. In early June keep a watchful eye overhead for Black Swift. Red-eyed Vireo are found in the cottonwoods along the river. For those looking for Wood Duck unsuccessfully in winter check along the river especially around the fish hatchery (green building) at the southwest corner of the lagoons. You may also drive back to Duncan, turning left at the traffic lights and drive to Boys Road (0.8 km). Just over the steel bridge you will see a Chinese restaurant. Behind the restaurant there are ponds that Wood Duck frequent during the winter months.

Duncan Sewage Lagoons to Somenos Creek

Retrace your route back to the junction of Lakes, Tzouhalem, and Trunk Roads, turning left onto Lakes Road (00.0 km.).

Somenos Creek

In winter, the flats along Somenos Creek harbour flocks of gulls and American Wigeon, occasionally a Eurasian Wigeon, or rarely Glaucous Gull. After driving (0.6 km.) turn left onto Beverly Street, then right onto a dirt road beside the golf driving range at the foot of York Road (1.0 km) (1.6 km.). This is an easy access to Somenos Creek close to Somenos Lake. The flooded grasses surrounding Somenos Creek during winter have produced American Bittern and Swamp Sparrow should also be found. The hedgerows and plowed fields in summer are productive.

Somenos Creek to Somenos Flats

Our last stop will be Somenos Flats. Proceed along Beverly Street to Highway 1 (0.5 km.) (2.1 km.) turning right for an additional (1.6 km.) (3.7 km.) and turn off the highway to the right at the nature centre. At the traffic lights on Highway 1 and Trunk Road in downtown Duncan, turn right towards Nanaimo along Highway 1 North. Drive (2.8 km) to metal gate and park.

Somenos Flats

Park outside the steel gate and walk along the wood walkway which leads to an delapidated bird blind. Along the walk you will pass two bird feeders that harbour Spotted Towhee, Fox Sparrow, Song Sparrow, Golden-crowned Sparrow, Dark-eyed Junco, House Finch and an occasional rare sparrow during winter. The fenceline has numerous nest-boxes which house a large population of Tree Swallow. This is possibly the best area to pick-up Black Swift. Scan the skies high overhead for migrants in early June when hundreds may be seen. As the swifts pass against the clouds both Black and Vaux's Swift may materialize. At other times through the summer Black Swift are erratic with storm fronts on Southern Vancouver Island. Migrants are seen in September but are not as prevalent here as in spring migration. This species migrates onto Vancouver Island north of the Saanich Peninsula, with only small numbers recorded there in spring. Sora and Common Snipe will be heard in the wet grasses surrounding the blind in summer. Black-crowned Night-Heron and American Bittern have been recorded and Blue-winged Teal frequently nest in the area. Marsh Wren are residents in the marsh and a small number of Swamp Sparrow spend the winter, listen for the sharp, metallic "chip". In winter the flooded areas support Trumpeter Swan and many other species of waterfowl including Gadwall, Eurasian Wigeon, Ring-necked Duck and Northern Shoveler.

MAP 11—COWICHAN VALLEY LOOP

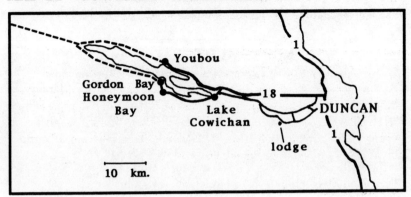

COWICHAN VALLEY LOOP

The Cowichan Valley is a long finger of the Southeast Coastal Lowlands that reaches deep into the East Coast zone, terminating at the east end of Cowichan Lake. Most Southeast Coastal Lowland species gradually decrease in number as one progresses up the valley with few found at the terminus at Youbou and Honeymoon Bay. Black-headed Grosbeak and fair numbers of Barred Owl are found around the perimeter of Cowichan Bay.

Victoria or Duncan to Gordon Bay Park

We start our trip at the Town and Country Shopping Centre on Highway 1 (Douglas Street) at Victoria (00.0 km.). After driving (61.3 km.) turn left onto Highway 18 West towards Lake Cowichan (5.6 km. north of Duncan). After driving an additional (25.7 km.) (87.0 km.) turn left to Lake Cowichan and Gordon Bay Park (well signed) keeping on South Shore Road to Honeymoon Bay. After an additional (13.2 km.) (100.2 km.) keep right on Walton Road at the sign for Gordon Bay Park for two more kilometers (102.2 km.).

Gordon Bay Park

Gordon Bay Park with 130 campsites is primarily a second-growth Douglas-fir forest with poor birding. The most abundant species are Hammond's Flycatcher (the most common empidonax around Cowichan Lake), Brown Creeper, Winter Wren, Golden-crowned Kinglet, Townsend's Warbler, and MacGillivray's

Warbler. Birding just outside the park in and around Honeymoon Bay is good, however, with the following general list of birds expected in summer.

KEY TO ABBREVIATIONS

A-abundant   C-common   R-rare   U-uncommon

Barred Owl U	Orange-crowned Warbler C
Rufous Hummingbird A	Yellow Warbler C
Red-breasted Sapsucker U	Yellow-rumped Warbler C
Northern Flicker C	Townsend's Warbler A
Olive-sided Flycatcher C	MacGillivray's Warbler C
Hammond's Flycatcher A	Wilson's Warbler U
Pacific-slope Flycatcher U	Western Tanager U
Tree Swallow U	Black-headed Grosbeak U
Violet-green Swallow C	Song Sparrow C
Steller's Jay C	White-crowned Sparrow U
Chestnut-backed Chickadee A	Dark-eyed Junco C
Winter Wren A	Brewer's Blackbird U
Swainson's Thrush A	Brown-headed Cowbird C
Varied Thrush U	Purple Finch U
Cedar Waxwing C	House Finch R
European Starling A	Red Crossbill U
Warbling Vireo C	Pine Siskin C
Evening Grosbeak R	

Gordon Bay Park to Lake Cowichan

(00.0 km.) On the trip back towards Lake Cowichan from Gordon Bay Park, turn left on Myers Road in Honeymoon Bay (1.8 km.). Black-headed Grosbeak should be heard singing in the willows along the edge of the lake. Other birds expected in season are Pacific-slope Flycatcher, Varied Thrush, Common Yellowthroat, Wilson's Warbler, Purple Finch and White-crowned Sparrow.

At Lake Cowichan stop at Saywell Park (11.4 km.) (13.2 km.). Between Saywell Park and the train trestle is a reliable site on the Cowichan River for Green Heron (across from the Green Heron Boutique!). A good spot to look from is atop the trestle. In the area you will encounter House Finch (common), Downy Woodpecker, and Killdeer nesting in the park.

Lake Cowichan to Duncan

After (1.2 km.) (14.4 km.) turn right along Cowichan Lake Road. Western Tanager and Hammond's Flycatcher are to be found for the next 22 kilometers. Notable stops for Western Tanager are (kms—16.4, 19.9, 21.4, 24.0). Some of the species found on the Southeast Coastal Lowlands appear along this stretch with California Quail, Bushtit, Bewick's Wren and Spotted Towhee.

After driving an additional (7.2 km.) (31.2 km.) turn right onto Skutz Falls Road which soon turns to gravel. Willow Flycatcher are found after (0.4 km.) (31.6 km.). It is (3.2 km.) (34.8 km.) to the falls where there is primitive camping. American Dipper are found easily along the river. Hammond's Flycatcher are abundant.

Retrace your route back to Cowichan Lake Road and turn right (00.0 km.). After (5.7 km.) you will have reached Stoltz Road which leads to Riverbottom Road. At 5720 Riverbottom Road is Sahtlam Lodge. Northern Saw-whet Owl are fairly reliable residents in the vicinity of the lodge. This uncommon resident is mainly found in damp areas on the Southeast Coastal Lowlands, primarily north of the Saanich Peninsula. It is a notable migrant in October when most recorded are injured or road-killed. In Sahtlam, an additional (2.4 km.) (8.1 km.) are Willow Flycatcher. This is basically the eastward limits for Hammond's Flycatcher in the valley. Pacific-slope Flycatcher now take over. After (4.2 km.) (12.3 km.) you will have reached Riverbottom Road. Turn right for the lodge if you missed the first road.

After another (4.0 km.) (16.3 km.) Cowichan Lake Road turns right. Then an additional (1.9 km.) (18.2 km.) (35.0 kilometers from the start of Cowichan Lake Road) and turn left onto Somenos Road for (2.4 km.) (20.6 km.) and turn right onto Highway 18. After driving (1.3 km) you will be back at Highway 1. Turn right for Duncan or Victoria or left for Nanaimo.

MAP 12—NANAIMO LOOP

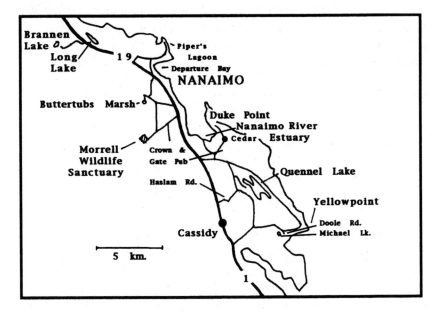

Brannen Lake · Long Lake · 19 · Piper's Lagoon · Departure Bay · NANAIMO · Buttertubs Marsh · Duke Point · Nanaimo River · Cedar · Estuary · Morrell Wildlife Sanctuary · Crown & Gate Pub · Quennel Lake · Haslam Rd. · Yellowpoint · Doole Rd. · Michael Lk. · Cassidy · 5 km. · 1

NANAIMO LOOP

Nanaimo lies at the northern parameter of the Southern Vancouver Island region. The area is reminiscent of the Saanich Peninsula with farms, woodlots and fields. The avifauna is homogeneous with the rest of Southern Vancouver Island. However, shorebirding is rather mundane with "rock" shorebirds isolated on offshore rocky islets. Black-throated Gray Warbler are especially numerous in the second-growth mixed and deciduous forests. Pied-billed Grebe remain to nest and American Coot remain later in spring and occasionally nest. American Bittern, found most readily here, may be found all year, although they are most common in winter.

The "specialities" here are feral American Black Ducks and Vancouver Island's only breeding colony of Vesper Sparrows.

American Black Duck were introduced some 25 years ago from introduced stock on the mainland in Mission and four separate introductions were made at the time in the Vancouver area. The populations stabilized on the year of introduction and have remained at approximately 70 individuals. The total population has not spread, confined to a very small region of Yellow Point—the parameters include an area approximately five by two kilometers. The entire range includes the Woodmont Farm ponds near Michael Lake, Quennell Lake, the Crow and Gate Pub's pond and a neighbouring pond. Rarely individuals stray south from this introduction site as far as Victoria where three remained for several years before disappearing. In recent years, individuals have strayed south annually to the Duncan area and north to Nanaimo. The total population revisits the introduction site at the Woodmont Farm on Doole Road each evening where they are fed and they may depend on this feeding during winter freeze-ups for survival. If this introduced population rely on this feeding for survival are they a viable "countable" population by ABA standards?

Nanaimo is 103 kilometers from Victoria along Highway 1 (Trans-Canada). It is also one of the main ferry ports from Vancouver.

Victoria or Duncan to Cassidy and Yellowpoint

Our trip starts from the Town and Country Shopping Plaza on Highway 1 (Douglas Street). It is an hour and a half drive to Nanaimo. After driving (84.6 km.) you will pass through Ladysmith on the 49th parallel. Soon after you will turn right at the sign for Cedar and Yellowpoint onto Cedar Road (5.0 km) (89.6 km). There are plenty of 24 hour gas stations en route from Victoria.

You may continue on Highway 1 for an additional (0.5 km.) (90.1 km.) to the southern edge of the Cassidy Airport. American Kestrel may be found during April on the wires beside the highway at the Cassidy Airport, usually north of the entrance—an additional (2.8 km.) (92.9 km). Vancouver Island's only Vesper Sparrow colony is located on the airport property, the only site for this extremely local breeding species. Between mid-April and early August at least six to eight singing males hold territory around the airport buildings, airplanes, and adjacent parimeter fenceline. Listen for the rich, melodious song that ends in varied trills.

Yellowpoint

Return to Cedar Road (00.0 km.). After driving (2.6 km.) along Cedar Road, continue straight ahead on Yellowpoint Road for the introductory site of the American Black Duck. After an additional (2.1 km.) (4.7 km.) turn right onto Doole Road and proceed to the wildfowl-fanciers ponds on the right (0.3 km.) (5.0 km). American Black Ducks should be found on the Woodmont Farm ponds at any time of the day throughout the year. If you arrive in the evening you are assured of seeing Vancouver Island's total population. At dusk the flock flies off to roost on nearby salt water, possibly at Kulieet Bay.

If you wish, you may proceed along Yellowpoint Road for the Yellowpoint Lodge which is an additional (3.8 km.). Yellowpoint Lodge is situated at the junction of Hills Road on 180 acres of natural oceanfront in typical lowland mixed forest.

The forest lacks large deciduous tracts and has most of the lowland species of this forest type including Western Screech-Owl, Great Horned Owl, Pileated Woodpecker, Pacific-slope Flycatcher, Chestnut-backed Chickadee, Red-breasted Nuthatch, Brown Creeper, Winter Wren, Golden-crowned Kinglet, Swainson's Thrush, American Robin, Varied Thrush (winter), Cassin's Vireo, Orange-crowned Warbler, Townsend's Warbler, Yellow-rumped Warbler, MacGillivray's Warbler, Wilson's Warbler, Spotted Towhee, Western Tanager, Song Sparrow, Dark-eyed Junco, Purple Finch, Red Crossbill and Pine Siskin. The oceanfront harbours many species of waterfowl in winter months, including both Black Scoter and Barrow's Goldeneye.

In brushy areas just outside the property are Rufous Hummingbird, Northern Flicker, Violet-green Swallow, Barn Swallow, Bushtit, Bewick's Wren and Chipping Sparrow. The odd House Wren is found along Yellowpoint Road about one kilometer past the American Black Duck site, where Savannah Sparrow and American Goldfinch frequent the grassy fields in summer.

Return to Cedar Road turning right (00.0 km.). Along Cedar Road you will find pleasant farmlands with Savannah Sparrow and Ring-necked Pheasant throughout. At (3.7 km.) turn left onto Haslam Road. You will find Pacific-slope Flycatcher and Black-throated Gray Warbler at the junction. At (0.4 km.) (6.7 km.) there is a small cattail marsh on the right with Sora and Virginia Rails. After (0.7 km.) (7.4 km.) check the wooded swamp on the night for Wood Ducks that have raised several families in recent years.

After (0.4 km) (7.8 km.) keep right at the fork for Haslam Road. After (0.9 km.) (8.7 km.) check again for Wood Duck. The small wet area on the airport property has shorebirds in spring migration, especially "peeps". The tract of large alders in this area have Pacific-slope Flycatcher, Warbling Vireo, Orange-crowned Warbler, Black-throated Gray Warbler and Wilson's Warbler. Red-eyed Vireo should be found in the area.

Retrace your route back to Cedar Road (00.0 km.), turning left. After driving (1.0 km.) turn right onto Quennell Road. Chipping Sparrow and Brewer's Blackbird are common in the memorial grounds at the junction. After (0.9 km.) (1.9 km.) pullover and check Quennell Lake. Quennell Lake is one of the few sites in the Nanaimo region where Trumpeter Swan winter. The odd Tundra Swan is found with these flocks. In summer, Common Yellowthroat sing from the brush. The handsome drake Gadwall and their plain mates often winter.

Return to Cedar Road and turn right (00.0 km.). After (1.3 km.) (or 8.6 from the corner of Cedar Road and Highway 1) turn right onto Yellow Point Road (follow the signs for the Crow and Gate Pub). After (1.5 km.) (7.5 km.) turn at the Crow and Gate Pub sign down their gravel entrance road for (0.2 km.) (7.7 km.). Directly in front of the pub is an artificial duck pond that supports a number of resident American Black Ducks throughout the day plus a few exotic farmyard duck species! The pub has excellent food and is well worth a stop for lunch.

(00.0 km.) After exiting the Crow and Gate Pub entrance Road, turn right and proceed along Yellowpoint Road to the town of Cedar (0.6 km.) (or 2.1 km. from the junction of Cedar and Yellowpoint Roads). In the town of Cedar, turn right onto MacMillan Road following the Harmac sign. You will immediately find York Lake, a small pond/marsh that has Trumpeter Swan, Green Heron, Virginia Rail, Marsh Wren, Yellow Warbler, Common Yellowthroat and Red-winged Blackbird. Green-winged Teal and Mallard are found seasonally.

Yellowpoint to the Nanaimo River Estuary

Return to Yellowpoint Road, turning right (00.0 km.). After driving (0.9 km.) you will come to a four-way junction. Continue straight ahead on Raines Road for the Nanaimo River Estuary (2.2 km.) (3.1 km.).

Nanaimo River Estuary

Along the road are Rufous Hummingbird on the overhead wires. In brushy areas are Bewick's Wren, Bushtit and White-crowned Sparrow. The alders along the river have Warbling Vireo, Yellow Warbler and Wilson's Warbler. On the river are Common Goldeneye, Belted Kingfisher and various gulls in season. Park at the terminus and walk the trail that is immediately after the gate on the right. In the upland areas there can be Short-eared Owl and (in invasion years) Snowy Owl, Snow Geese (in the fall), Western Meadowlark, Savannah Sparrow, Golden-crowned Sparrow and White-crowned Sparrow. Northern Shrike may also be encountered. The inter and high tidal areas yield the most diverse number of water species in the Nanaimo area. This is a wintering area for Horned Grebe, Pied-billed Grebe, Double-crested Cormorant, Pelagic Cormorant, Great Blue Heron, Trumpeter Swan, Canada Goose, Bufflehead, Common Goldeneye, Barrow's Goldeneye, Northern Pintail, Green-winged Teal, Mallard, Greater Scaup and Surf Scoter. Some of the raptors to be expected are Osprey, Bald Eagle, Northern Harrier (uncommon), Red-tailed Hawk, Merlin and Peregrine Falcon. The vagrant Swainson's Hawk has been recorded.

The tidal areas are quite a distance from the end of Raines Road and there are muddy channels laced throughout the area so appropriate footwear is advised, especially in winter months.

Nainaimo River Estuary to Duke Point

Return to the four-corner junction and turn left onto Harmac (Cedar) Road (00.0 km.). Continue for (1.0 km.) turning left at the 'T' junction towards Harmac on MacMillan Road. After (1.9 km.) (2.9 km.) the road forks at the Duke Point Industrial sign.

Duke Point

In the brush under the poles are MacGillivray s Warbler. Hutton's Vireo and Townsend's Warbler frequent the woods there.

Drive straight ahead along the left fork to its terminus (3.3 km.) (8.2 km.). At the terminus walk to the right and scope Northumberland Channel where Brandt's Commorant (in winter), Pelagic Comorant and Double-crested Comorant abound. Western Grebe, Horned Grebe, Red-necked Grebe, Common Loon and Pacific Loon will be found in winter with Rhinoceros Auklet, Marbled Murrelet and Pigeon Guillemot seasonally. On the short grassy areas and barren areas look for Horned Lark in the fall. The trees of the greenbelt often have Bald Eagle on their tops. The brush areas have California Quail, Rufous Hummingbird, Bushtit, Spotted Towhee, White-crowned Sparrow and Bewick's Wren.

Retrace your route back along MacMillan Road (00.0 km.). At (0.8 km.) pull over on the right and scope the Nanaimo River Estuarys mud flats at lower tides. Most of the common shorebirds will be seen seasonally. Purple Martins may be found nesting in the old pilings or seen during migrations. Cliff Swallow nest on the sandstone cliffs in the vicinity. In winter most of the common "saltchuck" ducks, loons, and grebes will be found, Western Grebe and Oldsquaw among them.

Duke Point to the Nanaimo Landfill

After (3.1 km.) (3.9 km.) turn right onto gravel Gordon Road. This is a pleasant quiet road to do some lowland birding. There is a nice wet area on the left after driving (1.3 km.) (5.2 km.). Common Snipe and Long-billed Dowitcher are to be expected. Solitary Sandpiper may be found.

After (0.2 km.) (5.4 km.) turn right onto Harmac Road, passing over a bridge after (0.6 km.) (6.0 km.) where Harmac changes name to Cedar Road. The Nanaimo landfill is on the left after (1.7 km.) (7.7 km.) which is open to the public—but ask for permission. Bald Eagle, Common Raven and Northwestern Crow are abundant. Glaucous-winged Gull is the abundant resident with other "dump" gulls seasonally, including an adult Iceland Gull among the Thayer's Gull recorded on November 28, 1992.

Nanaimo Landfill to Colliery Dam & Morrell Sanctuary

Continue along Cedar Road back to the Island Highway (Highway 1) and turn right (1.0 km.) (8.7 km.). After driving (1.0 km.) (9.7 km.) turn left at the traffic lights. You are now on 10th Street. Keep right after (0.3 km.) (10.0 km.). After an additional (2.1 km.) (12.1 km.) the road swings right and becomes Bruce Avenue. Proceed along Bruce Avenue and turn left onto 7th Street at the four-way stop (1.2 km.) (13.3 km.). Make a right onto Howard Avenue (0.4 km.) (13.7 km.), then a left onto Harewood Road (1.0 km.) (14.7 km.), then left after (0.5 km.) (1 5.2 km.) onto Wakesiah Road at the sign for Colliery Dam Park. Park at the parking lot at the bend in the road (0.2 km.) (15.4 km.). Colliery Dam Park has two lakes and lowland, mixed second-growth forest and is essentially the same habitat as Morrell Wildlife Sanctuary.

For more solitude, continue on to Morrell. Return to Harewood Road (now Nanaimo Lakes Road), turning left (0.2 km.) (15.6 km.) following the signs. Chipping Sparrow will be heard along the drive. After (1.2 km.) (16.8 km.) turn right into the sanctuary which is signed. Park at the parking lot (0.2 km.) (17.0 km.) where a map of the trails is displayed.

Morrell Wildlife Sanctuary

The Morrell Society have developed an excellent network of trails. Birdseed is set out in various locations throughout the trail system to ensure plenty of bird life. There are also several ponds and the largest has a viewing shelter.

This is a typical mixed lowland second-growth forest. The dominant warbler is the Black-throated Gray Warbler with Orange-crowned Warbler, Townsend's Warbler, MacGillivray's Warbler and Wilson's Warbler present. The dominant "empid" is the Pacitic-slope Flycatcher with the odd Hammond's Flycatcher in the purer stands of Douglas-fir. Other species to be expected include Band-tailed Pigeon, Red-breasted Sapsucker (mainly winter), Downy Woodpecker, Hairy Woodpecker, Pileated Woodpecker, Steller's Jay, Chestnut-backed Chickadee, Red-breasted Nuthatch, Winter Wren, Golden-crowned Kinglet, Swainson's Thrush, American Robin, Varied Thrush, Cassin's Vireo, Warbling Vireo, Hutton's Vireo, Spotted Towhee, Western Tanager, Fox Sparrow, Song Sparrow, Dark-eyed Junco, Purple Finch, Red Crossbill and Pine Siskin.

Morrell Sanetuary to Buttertubs Marsh

Return to Nanaimo Lakes Road, turning left (0.2 km.) (17.2 km.) and then left onto Wakesiah Road (1.1 km.) (18.3 km.). Proceed along Wakesiah Road turning left onto Jingle Pot Road (1.5 km.) (19.8 km.). Park on the side of the road opposite Addison Road (0.9 km.) (20.7 km.) for Buttertubs Marsh on the right.

Buttertubs Marsh

A broad gravel trail bisects the marsh. There are other trails that almost circle the marsh. The two ends of the trail come out to a road so a complete hike can be made around.

The variety of bird life here is incredible. American Bittern and Virginia Rail can be found throughout the year with Sora in the summer. The best place for the rails is the southern edge. Osprey, Merlin and Red-tailed Hawk will be seen in season. Tree Swallow, Violet-green Swallow, Northern Rough-winged Swallow, Cliff Swallow and Barn Swallow hawk over the marsh for insects. Yellow Warbler, Common Yellowthroat, Yellow-rumped Warbler, Orange-crowned Warbler and Wilson's Warbler will be found. Marsh Wren and Red-winged Blackbird are resident. On the Bowen Road side there are usually Mallards and Canada Geese waiting for handouts. Hooded Merganser nest in the lombardy poplars along the east side.

From the lookout tower on the broad gravel dike trail scan for Cinnamon Teal, Gadwall, Ring-necked Duck and Lesser Scaup, all seen on occasion. Great Blue Heron abound and lucky observers will find Green Heron. Pied-billed Grebe are resident and nest. American Coot are abundant and occasionally summer with rare nesting records. Common Snipe and Ring-necked Pheasants are found in the upland areas. Check the dead English oaks for Downy Woodpecker and Hairy Woodpecker. Cedar Waxwing and rarely Bohemian Waxwing can be seen in winter in the hawthorns. The scrub patches along the trails harbour California Quail, Rufous Hummingbird, Northern Flicker, Bushtit, Bewick's Wren, Ruby-crowned Kinglet, American Robin, Spotted Towhee, Fox Sparrow, Song Sparrow, Golden-crowned Sparrow, Dark-eyed Junco, Brown-headed Cowbird, House Finch and American Goldfinch in season. The brushy willow patches have Willow Flycatcher and taller deciduous scrub, Black-headed Grosbeak.

Buttertubs Marsh to Nanaimo and Departure Bay

Make a U turn and retrace your route back towards Nanaimo along Jingle Pot Road. At the traffic lights the name changes to Second Street. Continue straight ahead, turning left at Pine Street (1.8 km.) (22.5 km.). Make a right onto Bowen Road (double lane) after (0.5 km.) (23.0 km.), then left onto the Trans-Canada Highway (Highway 1) (0.8 km.) (23.8 km.). Immediately work your way over to the right following the signs for the Vancouver Ferry and turn right (0.2 km.) (24.0 km.). Here we will start at (00.0 km.). You are now on four-lane Stewart Avenue. It you continue ahead on the Trans-Canada (now Highway 19), you will find many fast-food and family restaurants, accommodations, and a visitors information centre (0.2 km.) on the right.

Continue on Stewart Avenue passing Nanaimo Harbour on the right. After (2.0 km.) keep to the left for a left turn following signs for Highway 19 and Parksville. If you wish to go to the ferry terminal, continue straight ahead.

After (0.9 km.) (2.9 km.) keep right onto Departure Bay Road. After (1.8 km.) (4.7 km.) pull off on the right to scope Departure Bay. Departure Bay is a good site for Mew Gull, Glaucous-winged Gull, Surf Scoter, White-winged Scoter and American Wigeon during the winter months. With a scope you can look out to Brannen Island for Black Oystercatcher which are common throughout the year.

Departure Bay to Piper's Lagoon Park

Continue along Departure Bay Road turning right onto Hammond Bay Road (0.3 km.) (5.0 km.). Follow Hammond Bay Road turning right onto Lagoon Road at the sign tor Piper's Lagoon (3.1 km.) (8.1 km.), then immediately right again onto Place Road, again following the signs.

Piper's Lagoon Park

Proceed to the parking lot of Piper's Lagoon Park (0.7 km.) (8.8 km.). Red-breasted Merganser, Barrow's Goldeneye and Harlequin Duck are often seen in the lagoon. Occasionally wintering shorebirds are numerous. Onshore in winter are the usual "saltchuck" species including Horned Grebe, Red-necked Grebe, Western Grebe, Common Loon, Pacific Loon, Double-crested Cormorant, Pelagic Cormorant, Surf Scoter, White-winged Scoter, Bufflehead, Common Merganser, Pigeon Guillemot and Marbled Murrelet. Black Oystercatcher may be also encountered.

From the point you may scope the distant Five Fingers Islets and Snake Island where there are breeding colonies of Double-crested Cormorant and Pelagic Cormorant, Glaucous-winged Gull, Black Oystercatcher and Pigeon Guillemot. "Rock" shorebirding is good on these isolated islets.

The point is an excellent area for Pileated Woodpecker, Bewick's Wren, Golden-crowned Kinglet, Ruby-crowned Kinglet, Spotted Towhee and vanous sparrows seasonally. Bald Eagle is often seen and Northwestern Crow are abundant.

Piper's Lagoon Park to Long and Brannen Lakes

Retrace your route, keeping right onto Departure Bay Road. At Departure Bay, turn right at (3.7 km.) (12.5 km.). Tum right onto Norwell Drive at (2.6 km.) (15.1 km.) and right onto Highway 19 at (1.2 km.) (16.3 km.). After driving (0.4 km.) (16.7 km.) turn off the highway into the Long Lake rest area. American Coot, Common Merganser, Hooded Merganser, Lesser Scaup, Mallard and Canada Goose are expected in winter months.

Continue along Highway 19 North turning left at the traffic lights at the Rutherford Village Mall onto Mostar Road (0.9 km.) (17.6 km.). Turn right immediately onto Metral Drive. Proceed along Metral Drive and turn left onto Godfrey Road at (0.6 km.) (18.2 km.) at the sign for Brannon Lake. After (0.5 km.) (18.7 km.) turn right at the four-way stop onto Dunster Road and park at the terminus (0.7 km.) (19.4 km.).

At Brannen Lake there are many species of wintering waterfowl with Pied-billed Grebe, Horned Grebe, Canada Goose, Mallard, Northern Shoveler, Canvasback, Lesser Scaup, Green-winged Teal, Hooded Merganser, Common Merganser and American Coot. Occasionally Ruddy Duck may be encountered. Cinnamon Teal and Blue-winged Teal could be found during their migration periods. Look for Lincoln's Sparrow in brushy areas during migration, especially during October-December. Willow Flycatcher and Black-headed Grosbeak occasionally frequent the brushy willow and taller brushy deciduous second-growth around the lake.

Brannen Lake, Nanaimo to Nanoose Bay

Return to Highway 19 and turn right for Nanaimo and Victoria or left for Parksville. In winter months, you may check Nanoose Bay en route to Parksville (approx. 25 km.) or (128.4 km.) from Victoria. Turn left into the rest area or right down Rumming Road (126.3 km. from Victoria). Nanoose Bay is a large bay clearly visible on the right side of the highway. The bay is the best site in the Nanaimo vicinity for Trumpeter Swan, Greater Scaup, Black Scoter, White-winged Scoter, Surf Scoter, Common Goldeneye, Barrow's Goldeneye, Bufflehead and Red-breasted Merganser. Common Loon and Pacific Loon and rarely Yellow-billed Loon are seen.

MAP 13—ROUTE 4 LOOP

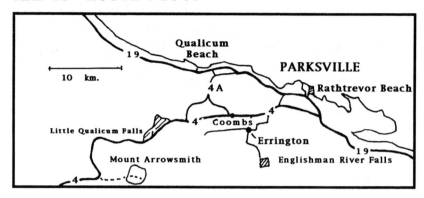

ROUTE 4 LOOP

Parksville

Parksville is 143 kilometers from Victoria on Highways 1 and 19—a 2 ½ hour drive. Parksville may be one of the best places to stay on Vancouver Island during the summer months. There are numerous motels, beautiful warm beaches, great restaurants, and many camping areas. The best park in the area for birders is Rathtrevor Beach Provincial Park situated (2.9 km.) south of Parksville on Highway 19 (0.5 km. south of the steel bridge and is well signed).

Another saltwater marsh is found adjacent to Rathtrevor at the Englishman River Estuary. Just south of the steel bridge turn east onto Plummer Road (a sharp left from Parksville) (00.0 km.). Drive (1.1 km.) where Plummer changes to Shorewood Drive, turn left (0.7 km.) (1.8 km.) onto Mariner Way. After an additional (0.6 km.) (2.4 km.) you will reach the marsh. Numerous ducks winter with Trumpeter Swan and the odd Eurasian Wigeon. There is a record of Ash-throated Flycatcher and Vancouver Island's only Little Blue Heron was photgraphed here.

Rathtrevor Beach Provincial Park

Rathtrevor Beach Provincial Park is very picturesque with its beautiful sandy beach and accompanying sand dunes and driftwood zone. Worth exploring are the wide variety of habitats with deciduous scrub, dry Douglas-fir forest, willow scrub, and a small marsh.

A checklist of the birds of Rathtrevor Beach Provincial Park and immediate area follows. Use the bar-graphs for Southern Vancouver Island to determine seasonal status. Black Swift are predictably seen over the park during summer.

Common Loon C
Pacific Loon A
Red-throated Loon U
Red-necked Grebe C
Horned Grebe C
Eared Grebe R
Western Grebe C
Double-crested Cormorant C
Brandt's Cormorant C
Pelagic Cormorant A
Great Blue Heron C
Canada Goose C
Brant A
Trumpeter Swan C
Mallard A
Northern Pintail C
Green-winged Teal C
Cinnamon Teal R
Blue-winged Teal U
American Wigeon A
Eurasian Wigeon R
Greater Scaup A
Common Goldeneye C
Barrow's Goldeneye C
Bufflehead A
Oldsquaw C
Harlequin Duck U
White-winged Scoter C
Surf Scoter A
Black Scoter C
Ruddy Duck R
Common Merganser C
Red-breasted Merganser C
Hooded Merganser C
Turkey Vulture C

Surfbird U
Black Turnstone U
Common Snipe C
Whimbrel U
Spotted Sandpiper C
Greater Yellowlegs C
Dunlin C
Western Sandpiper A
Red-necked Phalarope U
Red Phalarope R
Parasitic Jaeger U
Glaucous-winged Gull A
Thayer's Gull C
Herring Gull U
California Gull A
Ring-billed Gull U
Mew Gull A
Bonaparte's Gull A
Common Tern UC
Caspian Tern UR
Common Murre C
Pigeon Guillemot C
Marbled Murrelet C
Band-tailed Pigeon C
Mourning Dove R
Common Nighthawk C
Black Swift C
Vaux's Swift U
Rufous Hummingbird A
Belted Kingfisher C
Northern Flicker C
Pileated Woodpecker U
Red-breasted Sapsucker U
Hairy Woodpecker U
Downy Woodpecker C

Cooper's Hawk U
Sharp-shinned Hawk C
Red-tailed Hawk C
Bald Eagle C
Osprey U
Merlin U
Blue Grouse R
Ruffed Grouse U
Virginia Rail U
American Coot C
Semipalmated Plover C
Killdeer C
Pacific Golden-Plover R
American Golden-Plover R
Black-bellied Plover C
Brown Creeper C
House Wren R
Winter Wren C
Bewick's Wren C
Marsh Wren U R
American Robin A
Varied Thrush C
Hermit Thrush C
Swainson's Thrush A
Western Bluebird R
Golden-crowned Kinglet C
Ruby-crowned Kinglet C
American Pipit C
Cedar Waxwing C
Northern Shrike U
Eurasian Starling C
Hutton's Vireo U
Cassin's Vireo C
Warbling Vireo C
Orange-crowned Warbler C
Yellow Warbler C
Yellow-rumped Warbler C
Black-throated Gray Warbler U
Song Sparrow A
Lapland Longspur U

Hammond's Flycatcher UR
Willow Flycatcher R
Pacific-slope Flycatcher A
Olive-sided Flycatcher U
Horned Lark U
Violet-green Swallow A
Tree Swallow C
Barn Swallow C
Cliff Swallow U
Steller's Jay C
Common Raven C
Northwestern Crow A
Chestnut-backed Chickadee C
Bushtit U
Red-breasted Nuthatch C
Townsend's Warbler C
MacGillivray's Warbler C
Common Yellowthroat C
Wilson's Warbler C
House Sparrow C
Red-winged Blackbird C
Brewer's Blackbird C
Brown-headed Cowbird C
Western Tanager U
Evening Grosbeak U
Purple Finch C
House Finch U
Pine Siskin C
American Goldfinch C
Red Crossbill C
Spotted Towhee C
Savannah Sparrow C
Dark-eyed Junco A
Chipping Sparrow U
White-crowned Sparrow C
Golden-crowned Sparrow C
Fox Sparrow C
Lincoln's Sparrow C

Parksville to Qualicum Beach

(00.0 km.) North of Parksville on Highway 19 is the town of Qualicum Beach (10.9 km.) where the annual Brant Festival is held in April.

Black Scoters are abundant along the ocean front during winter. The Marshal-Stevenson or Qualicum National Wildlife Area is situated (3.6 km.) (14.5 km.) north of Qualicum Beach. The wildlife area has been closed to the public for some time but the marshes may be checked by turning right onto Kinkade Road (3.3 km.) north of Qualicum Beach or (14.2 km.) north of Parksville. Proceed along Kinkade Road, McFeely, and then Surfside Drive—a total of (1.2 km.) (15.3 km.) from Highway 19. In winter the marsh has ducks and many Bald Eagle frequent the moss-draped Douglas-fir snags. Canada's only Thick-billed Kingbird was seen in this vicinity during October and November of 1974. As with many vagrants, the kingbird eventually starved when it could not find enough flying insects during cold weather. There is a record of Snowy Plover from the adjacent beach and Caspian Tern erratically frequent this beach.

Parksville to Englishman River Falls Park

Highway 4 may be reached from downtown Parksville or from a by-pass south of Parksville. From the beginning of the by-pass, drive (5.9 km.) merging off at the Parksville/Errington exit. Turn left under the overpass, then right onto Highway 4. From downtown Parksville it is (1.9 km.) to this jumction.

(00.0 km.) From the the above junction drive (3.1 km.) along Highway 4 and turn left at the sign for Englishman River Falls Park. The paved road passes through Errington and on to the park (9.0 km.) (12.1 km.).

Englishman River Falls Park

Most "forest" species are present within the park including Northern Flicker, Red-breasted Sapsucker, Pileated Woodpecker, Hammond's Flycatcher, Chestnut-backed Chickadee, Red-breasted Nuthatch, Brown Creeper, Winter Wren, Townsend's Warbler and Dark-eyed Junco. American Dipper frequents the falls.

In the farms, fields, and mixed second-growth forest outside of the park are Band-tailed Pigeon, Common Nighthawk, Rufous

Hummingbird, Blue Grouse, Hairy Woodpecker, Pacific-slope Flycatcher, Steller's Jay, Common Raven, Bewick's Wren, Swainson's Thrush, Cedar Waxwing, Cassin's Vireo and Western Tanager.

Englishman Falls/Qualicum Beach to Hamilton Swamp

Retrace your route back to Highway 4 and turn left towards Coombs (00.0 km.). After driving (3.9 km.) you will arrive in Coombs, an interesting touristy stop with its sod-roofed shops. Proceed along Highway 4. After an additional (4.6 km.) (8.5 km.) turn right onto Highway 4A. Proceed along 4A for (1.1 km.) (9.6 km.), turning right following the signs for Qualicum Beach. Another left turn follows. After driving (3.3 km.) (12.9 km.) from Highway 4 you will find a small parking area on the right—Hamilton Swamp. Hamilton Swamp may also be reached along Highway 4A from downtown Qualicum Beach—just follow signs for Port Alberni and Tofino or Highway 4. It is (5.1 km.) to Hamilton Swamp (on left) from Qualicum Beach.

Hamilton Swamp is a cedar-alder bottomland with a large vegetated marsh. The better birds found here include Barred Owl and Northern Saw-whet Owl. The salal undergrowth, where the forest is more open, offers habitat for MacGillivray's Warbler. An unconfirmed record of a Chestnut-sided Warbler exists (July 1982).

Hamilton Swamp to Mount Arrowsmith Ski Area

Return to Highway 4, turning right towards Port Alberni (00.0 km.). Along the route you will pass several parks. Little Qualicum Falls Park (with camping facilities) is reached after driving an additional (4.4 km.) or (16.3 km.) from Parksville. The gate is (0.3 km.) from the highway. The park is mainly Douglas-fir mixed with a few arbutus. There are deciduous trees in the lower campground. Birds typical of lowland second-growth mixed forest are found here including Hammond's Flycatcher. Beauford Provincial Park is on the east end of Cameron Lake an additional (6.7 km.) (11.5 km.) or (23.0 km.) from Parksville.

Proceed west along Highway 4 towards Port Alberni. After an another (3.4 km.) (14.9 km.) you will drive through Cathedral Grove, a remnant patch of towering, monolithoic old-growth forest. High overhead sunlight penetrates the canopy in a cathedral manner, filtering beams of silky light across immense trunks. Nothing rivals the giant ancient Douglas-firs, walking among them is an experience few people will forget. Birding, however, is poor.

After another (8.6 km.) (23.5 km.) you will pass the entrance to Mount Arrowsmith Ski Area on the left. At the summit, White-tailed Ptarmigan and Gray Jay are to be found. The Mount Arrowsmith ski area is (35.0 km.) from Parksville. It is (17.5 km.) to the ski area on fair gravel road from Highway 4. From Highway 4, turn left (00.0 km.). At (2.6 km.) make a left turn (this road to the summit is only open to the public on weekends!). At kilometers 5.5, 8.2, 9.5, 5.8, 10.4 and 13.5 keep left. There are usually ski signs at these junctions. The last 10 kilometers are fairly steep and the road clings to perilously vertical heights (not for those with vertigo!).

Mount Arrowsmith Ski Area

At (17.5 km.) pull off on the wide area, you will be at a sharp left turn. An old spur logging road (not drivable) leads up the south-side of a logged valley. You will see the alpine ridges about 600' above. At the end of the spur road, a trail leads to the summit of Mount Arrowsmith at 5,962 ft. It is a strenuous hike, but it is the shortest walk to see the ptarmigan on Vancouver Island, about two hours one-way.

The views are magnificent! The lichen-dominated alpine of these wind-swept ridges are still snow-covered into June. It is best to look for the ptarmigan in August when most of the snow has melted and the parent birds are less secretive, protecting their young. The White-tailed Ptarmigan are most often found in rocky areas above timberline on these wind-blown ridges; the ptarmigan are scarcer here than on Forbidden Plateau, however. The ptarmigan may be difficult to locate because of their abilities of camouflage. Search the rubble areas where their mottled summer plumage will make them close to invisible, sit still and watch for movement.

If you drive too far along the road towards the ski area, you will come to a yellow metal gate on the right, exactly an additional (1.0 km.) (18.5 km.). Gray Jay and Blue Grouse are common along the gated road and lucky observers have found Three-toed Woodpecker. Return to Highway 4, turning left for Port Alberni. It is an additional (15.0 km.), a total of (50 km.) from Parksville or (193 km.) from Victoria.

MAP 14—PORT ALBERNI

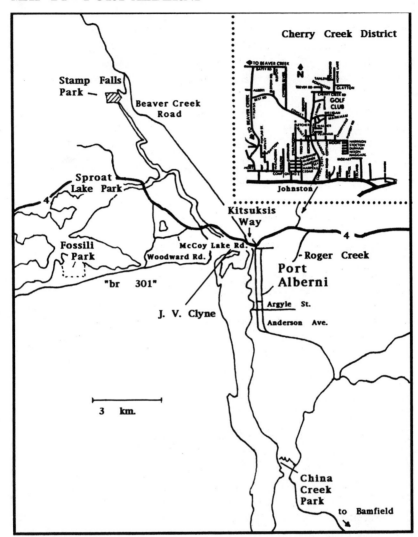

Port Alberni

Port Alberni lies within an isolated area of the Southeast Coastal Lowlands bio-geoclimatic zone known as the Alberni Lowlands. The status of birds in the Alberni Lowlands is homogenous with that of the northern sector of the Southeast Coastal Lowlands except that the isolation limits the number of "lowland specialities".

Port Alberni is unique in that it is the only large settlement lying close to the dividing edge of the east and west coast bio-geoclimatic zones. It is unusual in having a great arm of the Pacific Ocean that reaches deep into the interior of the Island. This inlet, Alberni Inlet, terminates at Port Alberni giving it a flavour of west coastal birding with a record of Fork-tailed Storm-Petrel occuring this far "inland". A few Black Turnstone and Surfbird (occasionally numerous) are seen in winter and during migrations. Black Swift will be seen flying over their area in summer and Common Nighthawk over the city.

The "Green Pheasant" (Phasianus colchicus versicolor), an introduced Japanese form of the Ring-necked Pheasant is found fairly commonly here, the only "specality".

Cherry Creek

As you enter town along Highway 4 you will pass Cherry Creek Road on your right (3.0 km) past the I.G C. liquid gas station (see Port Alberni map). Cherry Creek, reminiscent of the Saanich Peninsula because of the rural houses, farms, woodlots, and homesteads often gravitates local rarities to the area of Port Alberni. Examples are Snow Goose, Eurasian Wigeon, Gyrfalcon and Townsend's Solitaire. Merlin, Northern Shrike, Evening Grosbeak and Red Crossbill may be found seasonally. Return to Highway 4 into downtown Port Alberni and the 'T' junction at the traffic lights at Johnston Street.

Port Alberni to Stamp Falls Provincial Park

(00.0 km.) Turn right at the stoplights from the corner of the Alberni Highway (Highway 4) and Johnston Street to continue along Highway 4 West. After (0.3 km.) turn right onto Beaver Creek Road at the sign for Stamp Falls Provincial Park. After an additional (12.5 km.) (12.8 km.) turn left following the sign to Stamp Falls Provincial Park. After an additional (1.7 km.) (14.5 km.) you will reach the park.

Stamp Falls Provincial Park

Birding is rather poor in the mixed second-growth forest. Hammond's Flycatcher, Swainson's Thrush, Townsend's Warbler and Cassin's Vireo are very common. At the falls are American Dipper with Common Merganser and Belted Kingfisher along the river. Common residents include Chestnut-backed Chickadee, Winter Wren, Golden-crowned Kinglet, Varied Thrush and Dark-eyed Junco. Common

Yellowthroat are found at the marshy section near the park entrance where Common Snipe are heard winnowing in the twilight hours of summer.

Stamp Falls Provincial Park to Toad Lake

From Stamp Falls Provincial park continue along Beaver Creek Road (which changes name) staying on the main paved road for an additional (6.7 km.) (19.2 km.) from the beginning of Beaver Creek Road. At the small "Trout for Sale" sign on the right, turn left onto the gravel logging road resetting your odometer to (00.0 km). The road is open all week to traffic and may be travelled through to Courtney but is quite rough along Comox Lake. Along the drive you will be within the Eastern Vancouver Island or East Coast Zone where Red-breasted Sapsuckers are common especially around beaver ponds and other lakes.

The road has a few potholes for the first stretch, but soon improves. After a short distance you will see an orange gate on the right. Continue ahead on the main road. After (2.3 km.) (3.3 km.) keep left on the main road. At (3.7 km.) keep right at the junction where the road will improve. At (9.3 km) keep left on the main road. At (10.2 km.) turn right where there is a small white sign "Comox" (the road at this point going straight ahead is not the main road!). At (11.0 km.) keep right and at (15.6 km.) keep right again along the main road. At (17.4 km.) is a small lake on the right and at (18.1 km.) and (20.5 km.) are small bridges. At (22.2 km.) you will see Toad Lake on the left. At (22.9 km.) are two red metal posts, one on each side of the road. During May 1994, a pair of Hermit Warblers (a hybrid male and pure female) were discovered here. Speculation arose as to the possibility of more Hermits in the area but further sightings have not occurred. Check south along the road from Toad Lake, especially in the first eight kilometers for Red-breasted Sapsuckers. Blue Grouse are very common with the odd Ruffed Grouse and Western Tanager. Townsend's Warblers are abundant.

Beaver Creek Road

Returning back to Beaver Creek Road, turn right (00.0 km.) towards Port Alberni. Birding along Beaver Creek Road is very productive offering a wide mixture of lowland habitat. Warbling Vireo are common throughout. Hammond's Flycatcher are found from (kms. 0—3) replacing the Pacific-slope Flycatcher which is scarce in the Alberni Lowlands. Orange-crowned Warbler are found at

(0.6 km.) with Black-throated Gray Warbler and Willow Flycatcher between (1.6 –2.0 km.). Western Tanager are fairly common from (2.5—4.5 km.). Willow Flycatcher are again found between (5.5—6.3 km) where the fields should be checked for "Green" Pheasant. Regular Ring-necked Pheasant will also be encountered. In summer expect to see Rufous Hummingbird, Violet-green Swallow, Barn Swallow, Cedar Waxwing, White-crowned Sparrow and American Goldfinch. Resident Red-tailed Hawk, Red-breasted Sapsucker (uncommon), Downy Woodpecker, Northern Flicker, Steller's Jay, Chestnut-backed Chickadee, Bushtit, Red-breasted Nuthatch, Hutton's Vireo (uncommon), Spotted Towhee, Song Sparrow, House Finch, Red-winged Blackbird, Brewer's Blackbird, Purple Finch and Pine Siskin. In winter you may encounter Northern Shrike and rarely Northern Harrier.

Back in Port Alberni (3.7 km.) (12.0 km.) is a small marsh just across from Beaver Creek Gardens with Yellow Warbler and Green Heron. Black-headed Grosbeak is rare but possible here. To thoroughly check for the herons, arrive early in the morning. After an additional (0.4 km.) (12.4 km.) pull into the Alberni Athletic Hall parking lot and walk Kitsuksis Way, the pathway along the river, looking for herons, or check around the Clutesi Marina on Albemi Inlet over Highway 4. A careful check should produce one. In winter the marina should produce Red-throated Loon, Pelagic Cormorant (uncommon), Mallard, American Wigeon, Greater Scaup, Common Goldeneye, Bufflehead, Common Merganser, Hooded Merganser, Mew Gull, Glaucous-winged Gull and Belted Kingfisher. California Gull are found in summer and fall.

Beaver Creek Road to Roger Creek and Alberni Inlet

Retrace your route back to Port Alberni to the lights at Highway 4 West and Johnston Street (Alberni Highway), turn left (towards Parksville) for (0.1 km.), then right on Gertrude Street. On the left (0.5 km.) you will see the Barclay Pacific Hotel. The adjacent deciduous woods have produced Red-eyed Vireo (June 1988). Proceed along Gertrude Street which changes name to Stamp Avenue, then to Third Avenue. After an additional (0.8 km.) (a total of 1.3 km. from Johnston Street) you may turn left on Redford Street to return to Parksville via the Port Alberni Highway, stopping at the Roger Creek Nature Trail—step 74 (1.7 km.) (3.0 km.). Pull into the parking lot on the right. Here in the mixed second-growth bottomland you may find Black-throated Gray Warbler, Hammond's Flycatcher and many of the common birds associated with this habitat. It you proceed right from the parking lot it is an additional (1.5 km.) (4.5 km.) to Highway 4.

You may also reach China Creek Park (at the edge of the east-west coast bio-geoclimatic zones) by turning left at Redford Street, then right at 10th Avenue following the signs for Bamfield. After (1.2 km.) you may turn right on Argyle Street to its termination at Alberni Inlet (1.3 km.). During winter the inlet has Red-throated Loon, Pacific Loon, Common Loon, Horned Grebe (uncommon), Red-necked Grebe, Western Grebe, Double-crested Cormorant, Pelagic Cormorant (uncommon), Greater Scaup, Surf Scoter, Common Goldeneye, Bufflehead and Common Merganser. "Rock" shorebirds will be encountered rarely on rocky areas. Mew Gull, Glaucous-winged Gull, California Gull and other gull species will be recorded seasonally.

Port Alberni to China Creek Park

To proceed to China Creek Park, turn left at Argyle Street (see above) at the sign for Bamfield. After (0.2 km.) turn right onto Anderson (sign to China Creek and Bamfield). After an additional (2.1 km.) turn left on Ship Creek Road which soon turns to gravel. Be sure and gas-up and check your spare tire before this trip. Hammond's Flycatcher will be found along this sector of road especially on the short stretch of pavement. After driving (4.8 km.) turn right at the sign for China Creek—Franklin River- Bamfield. Warbling Vireo, Cassin's Vireo and Hammond's Flycatcher will be heard driving this rather rough section of road which is passable with a passenger car. After driving an additional (4.7 km.) keep left at the sign for Bamfield. Then an additional (1.6 km.) and turn right to China Creek Park (1.1 km.) (a total of 12.2 km. from pavement at Port Alberni)

China Creek Park

The park has 260 camping sites but is usually deserted. In the park and at the inlet in summer expect Common Merganser, Spotted Sandpiper, Swainson's Thrush, Warbling Vireo, Townsend's Warbler and MacGillivray's Warbler. Blue Grouse are common in the forests just outside the park. On the inlet during the winter months are Common Murre, Marbled Murrelet and numerous salt waterfowl including Barrow's Goldeneye,

You may carry on to Bamfield (approximately 60 km.) or to Lake

Cowichan via Franklin River Camp (105.1 km.) (all of which have gas). Travel to these locations is all on logging road.

Beaver Creek Road to Airport and J.V. Clyne Sanctuary

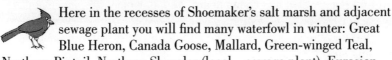 At Highway 4 West (River Road), turn right towards Pacific Rim (0.2 km.) (12.6 km.). After driving an additional (3.0 km.) (15.6 km.) you will cross over a bridge. Turn left onto Mission Road at the sign for the airport (00.0 km.). Follow the river for (0.6 km.). Here the road forks and changes to gravel. Follow the river and the airport signs to the airport (0.4 km.) (1.0 km.). At the Port Alberni Airport rarities such as Northern Harrier, Short-eared Owl and Western Meadowlark have been found. Whimbrel and Savannah Spanow are to be found in migration.

Return to Mission Road (now a logging road) and turn left, keeping left at Rowe Road. After driving an additional (1.0 km.) (2.0 km.) turn left down the dirt road at the sign designating the J.V. Clyne Nature Santuary (0.8 km.) (2.8 km.).

J.V. Clyne Nature Sanctuary

Here in the recesses of Shoemaker's salt marsh and adjacent sewage plant you will find many waterfowl in winter: Great Blue Heron, Canada Goose, Mallard, Green-winged Teal, Northern Pintail, Northern Shoveler (local—sewage plant), Eurasian Wigeon (rare), American Wigeon, Common Goldeneye and Bufflehead. In migration both Blue-winged Teal and Cinnamon Teal (rare) have been recorded. In the nearby brush and marsh vegetation are resident Downy Woodpecker, Steller's Jay, Northwestern Crow, Chestnut-backed Chickadee, Bewick's Wren (uncommon), Winter Wren, Golden-crowned Kinglet, Spotted Towhee, Song Sparrow and Purple Finch. In winter months at least one Marsh Wren will be encountered in the marsh. Shorebirding is fair with resident Killdeer and Common Snipe which are prevalent during the winter. Migrants that may be seen include Black-bellied Plover, Semipalmated Plover, Greater Yellowlegs, Spotted Sandpiper, Least Sandpiper, Western Sandpiper, Dunlin, Short-billed Dowitcher and Long-billed Dowitcher. In winter months numerous Trumpeter Swan will be seen to the east in fields beyond the obvious pipe. Bald Eagle, Mew Gull and Glaucous-winged Gull will also be present in winter. For further access to Shoemaker Bay return to, and turn left, on Mission Road following this gravel logging road for an additional (1.1 km.)—stopping where there is a closed gate. If you wish to do some "owling", turn right off the logging road (Mission Road) just before the locked gate at (0.8 km.) where there is a sign for McTush.

J.V. Clyne to McCoy Lake, owling sites and Fossili Park

Access to the "owling" area may be reached from Highway 4. Return to Highway 4 West, turning left (00.0 km.). Proceed along Highway 4 for (0.5 km.) turning left onto McCoy Lake Road. After an additional (2.0 km.) (2.5 km.) you will see McCoy Lake on the right which has many Lesser Scaup and American Coot in the winter months along with a few Ruddy Duck, Ring-necked Duck and Pied-billed Grebe. A scope is best as the lake is a distance away. Brewer's Blackbird and Ring-necked Pheasant are resident here.

For those wishing to see Wood Duck (local—summer) and for owling, turn left onto gravel Woodward Road after (0.4 km.) (2.9 km.). After (0.4 km.) (3.3 km.) you will reach a pipe passing under the road. Here both Barred Owl and Western Screech-Owl have been enticed to call using a tape. Continue up the road. After an additional (1.6 km.) (4.9 km.) you will come to a "T" junction at a gravel pit. Here both Barred Owl and Northern Pygmy-Owl have been heard. You may turn right for Shoemaker Bay or for Fossili Park where Wood Duck nest. Drive (3.9 km.) (8.8 km.) to an overgrown road with a sign "BR 301" on the right. Continue on BR 301 for an additional (0.5 km.) (9.3 km.) to a small parking lot. From here it is a half hour hike into the park crossing a suspension bridge and following St. Andrews Creek to an alder flat. The beaver pond is shortly beyond the flats. Blue Grouse should be found along Woodward Road during summer with Pileated Woodpecker and Hairy Woodpecker in the vicinity of the gravel pit.

Sproat Lake Provincial Park

(00.0 km.) Back at Highway 4 (Sproat Lake) turn left. After driving (6.6 km.) turn right at Central Lake Road for Sproat Lake Provincial Park. At the corner of Highway 4 West and Central Lake Road are Willow Flycatcher. Immediately turn left to the entrance of the park which is signed. The park has 59 campsites. The mixed forest is more deciduous than Stamp Falls with some willow scrub. Winter Wren, Steller's Jay, Swainson's Thrush, Townsend's Warbler and MacGillivray's Warbler are abundant during summer. Rufous Hummingbird, Hammond's Flycatcher and Cassin's Vireo are to be expected.

Return to Highway 4, turn right, and drive an additional (0.5 km.) (7.1 km.). Turn left at Lakeshore Road, then immediately left again for the lakeshore side of Sproat Lake Provincial Park. There is good birding here with Black-throated Gray Warbler and Warbling Vireo. Other expected species include: Pileated Woodpecker, Hammond's Flycatcher, Chestnut-backed Chickadee, Winter Wren, Swainson's Thrush, Townsend's Warbler, Spotted Towhee and Dark-eyed Junco.

Port Alberni to Long Beach

At Port Alberni (193 km from Victoria), turn right at the traffic lights at Highway 4 and Johnston Street for Highway 4 West towards Tofino. It is an additional 91 kilometers to the junction of Highway 4 West and the begining of Pacific Rim National Park (a total of 284 km.), a 4½ to 5 hour drive from Victoria. Here you may turn left towards Ucluelet (8 km.) or right to Long Beach and Tofino (34 km.).

Along the drive from Port Alberni you will pass Taylor Arm Park (without camping) and Sproat Lake Park (with camping). Stop to see the small falls and rapids at Kennedy River, which runs along Highway 4. Check here for Amencan Dipper (rare). Overnight facilities, grocery stores, restaurants, and gas stations are to be found at Parksville, Port Alberni, Tofino, and Ucluelet.

MAP 15—LONG BEACH

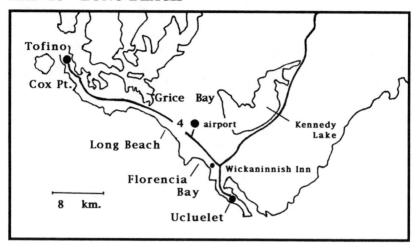

PACIFIC RIM NATIONAL PARK (LONG BEACH)

Pacific Rim National Park, along with Jordan River and Port Renfrew, are the only stretches of the west coast which are easily accessed and the only sites that may be driven to on paved road. Pacific Rim National Park is reached by driving (143 km.) north and west from Victoria along Highways 1 and 19, then taking the Port Alberni (Tofino) cutoff just before Parksville. Follow the new highway and signs for Port Alberni and/or Long Beach for approximately 20 kilometers, taking the exit which will lead you to Highway 4 west of Coombs. Follow the signs right (west) towards Port Alberni.

Many species of birds found on the east coast of Vancouver Island are lacking on its west coast, although a few species are found more readily here in summer months when most travellers visit the island. Fox Sparrow should be seen along McLean Point Road and Steller's Jay throughout the park. Hermit Thrush may be encountered. Often Black-legged Kittiwake can be seen on the sand beaches especially after strong onshore winds. Western Gull and Herring Gull are uncommon residents. Scanning from the shore, Tufted Puffin, Sooty Shearwater, Red-throated Loon and Pacific Loon may be seen. However, to be sure of seeing Tufted Puffin a pelagic trip is necessary. Although this bizzare bird might be encountered on one of the boat trips available to see whales and sea-lions, these boats do not go far enough offshore to see pelagics. Ancient Murrelet may also be seen from the whale-watching boats, a rare, regular summer visitor.

For inshore excursions contact:
Whale Watching Tours
Inter-lsland Excursions, Box 393, Tofino, B.C. VOR 2Z0

For pelagic trips contact:
Intertidal Tours, Ucuelet, B.C.
(604) 726-7336 (business)

Three shorebirds seen more readily in transit at Long Beach include Whimbrel, with large flocks on the beaches in May, and Wandering Tattler on the surf-washed rocks. A good site for Wandering Tattler is the rocky shoreline of Cox Point or north of there along the rocky Tofino shoreline. Red Knot may be encountered in good numbers during migrations, especially in May. The Snowy Plover is exceptionally rare (four records) but the lucky birder may chance upon one on the sandy beaches in April through June.

In the fall, usually September and early October, there are organized trips off the west coast to look for pelagics. These occassional trips will be advertised on the Victoria rare Bird Alert. The trips leave from Ucluelet or Tofino in moderately-sized and very comfortable boats. Trips can be taken at almost anytime of the year (when weather permits) with Intertidal Tours using fast, but small, open Zodiac craft.

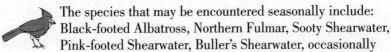

The species that may be encountered seasonally include: Black-footed Albatross, Northern Fulmar, Sooty Shearwater, Pink-footed Shearwater, Buller's Shearwater, occasionally Flesh-footed Shearwater and Short-tailed Shearwater. Fork-tailed Storm-Petrel, rarely Leach's Storm-Petrel, Cassin's Auklet, Tufted Puffin, Red Phalarope, Red-necked Phalarope, occasionally Long-tailed Jaeger, Parasitic Jaeger and Pomarine Jaeger. Individual South Polar Skua are encountered with variable numbers of Black-legged Kittiwake, Sabine's Gull and occasionally Arctic Tern. Other much rarer species have been seen such as Black-vented Shearwater, Laysan Albatross (October) and Thick-billed Murre.

The birding coverage of this region is slight with few active resident birders and park naturalists only during summer. Many visitors bird here before and after pelagic trips, often adding species to the ever-growing checklist of 286 species of which 54 are breeding residents. Many very rare species have been discovered in the park and area despite the scant coverage, among them Great Egret, Emperor Goose, Ross's Goose, American Avocet, Hudsonian Godwit, Bar-tailed Godwit, Curlew Sandpiper, Elegant Tern, Horned Puffin, Great Gray Owl, White-winged Dove, Ash-throated Flycatcher, Tropical Kingbird, Scissor-tailed Flycatcher, Blue Jay, Blue-gray Gnatcatcher, Brown Thrasher, wagtail species, Bay-breasted Warbler, Hooded Warbler, Dickcissel, Clay-colored Sparrow, Lark Sparrow, Chestnut-collared Longspur, Rustic Bunting, McKay's Bunting, Bobolink, Common Grackle and Brambling. A Falcated Duck was present for two consecutive winters, but as with any waterfowl, the species is kept in captivity and counting it as a true vagrant is left to the observer (the ABA discounts this species outside of Alaska). An Oriental Turtle-Dove was present during August 1992. The unusual summer occurance, plus the fact that this species is known to be kept as a caged species on the island leads to doubts as to its origin.

Pacific Rim National Park Trails

The following trails are marked within park boundaries. The species listed are those most likely to be encountered: Caspian Tern are often seen in numbers (erratic) on all of the beaches.

McLean Point Road (78 species)

Winter	*All Year*
Common Loon	Glaucous-winged Gull
Red-necked Grebe	Song Sparrow
Western Grebe	Golden-crowned Kinglet
Greater Scaup	Dark-eyed Junco
Bufflehead	Varied Thrush
Surf Scoter	Winter Wren

Summer	*Migration*
Band-tailed Pigeon	Whimbrel
Rufous Hummingbird	Yellow-rumped Warbler
Northern Flicker	
Pacific-slope Flycatcher	
Chestnut-backed Chickadee	
American Robin	

Summer, cont.
Swainson's Thrush
Orange-crowned Warbler
Common Yellowthroat
Fox Sparrow

Grice Bay Trail (57 species)
Winter   *All Year*
Trumpeter Swan   Chestnut-backed Chickadee
Mallard   Winter Wren
Sanderling   Golden-crowned Kinglet
Red Crossbill   American Robin
                                   Song Sparrow

Summer
Band-tailed Pigeon
Rufous Hummingbird
Pacific-slope Flycatcher
Steller's Jay
Northwestern Crow
Swainson's Thrush
Townsend's Warbler
Orange-crowned Warbler

The best mudflats for shorebirds is at Grice Bay with Long-billed
Dowitcher and Short-billed Dowitcher and the expected species associated with this habitat (see West Coast column 1 on the checklist).

Rain Forest Trail (16 species)
Summer   *All Year*
Steller's Jay   Winter Wren
Pacific-slope Flycatcher   Golden-crowned Kinglet
Red Crossbill
Swainson's Thrush   *Uncommon Species*
                                   Pileated Woodpecker
                                   Brown Creeper

Florencia Bay Lookout (56 species)
Summer
Northern Rough-winged Swallow frequent the banks

Fall/Winter
Common Loon
Pacific Loon
Western Grebe
Harlequin Duck
Surf Scoter
Glaucous-winged Gull
Heermann's Gull
Black-legged Kittiwake
Pigeon Guillemot
Marbled Murrelet
Belted Kingfisher

Uncommon Species
Red-throated Loon
Sooty Shearwater
Osprey
Black Oystercatcher
Ancient Murrelet
Rhinoceros Auklet
Tufted Puffin
Whimbrel

Goldmine Trail (39 species)
Summer
Band-tailed Pigeon
Rufous Hummingbird
Northern Flicker
Swainson's Thrush
Orange-crowned Warbler
White-crowned Sparrow
Wilson's Warbler
American Robin
Song Sparrow

Uncommon Species
Blue Grouse
Vaux's Swift
Willow Flycatcher
Olive-sided Flycatcher
MacGillivray's Warbler

All Year
Steller's Jay
Winter Wren

Swan Lake (46 species)
Summer
Mallard
Wood Duck
Common Nighthawk
Rufous Hummingbird
Pacific-slope Flycatcher
Olive-sided Flycatcher
Tree Swallow
Northern Rough-winged Swallow

Uncommon Species
Pied-billed Grebe
Trumpeter Swan
Blue-winged Teal
Ring-necked Duck
Hooded Merganser

Arnerican Robin
Swainson's Thrush
Cedar Waxwing
Orange-crowned Warbler
Song Sparrow

Willowbrae Trail (30 species)

Summer	*All Year*
Pacific-slope Flycatcher	Chestnut-backed Chickadee
Steller's Jay	Golden-crowned Kinglet
Northwestern Crow	
Winter Wren	*Uncommon Species*
Swainson's Thrush	Brown Creeper
Townsend's Warbler	Hutton's Vireo

Other birding sites include the Tofino Airport, signed between Wickaninnish and Tofino, and the sewage ponds near the Wickaninnish Inn (also signed at the beginning of the Pacific Rim Highway). The airport has many brushy and open areas that attract raptors and Golden-crowned Sparrows during migration through the winter months. White-crowned Sparrow are resident but scarce during winter. Observers may find Western Meadowlark and other rarities that are attracted to the area. The sewage ponds (1.1 km.) towards Tofino on the left past the Wickaninnish Inn turnoff have produced several rare birds during fall migration lately, among them Chestnut-sided and Bay-breasted Warblers.

A rather famous bird-feeder is present in downtown Tofino that has attracted Oriental Turtle-Dove and Rustic Bunting as well as several local rarities. Phone the Victoria Rare Bird Alert to see if any rare birds may be present.

MAP 16—COURTENAY—COMOX LOOP

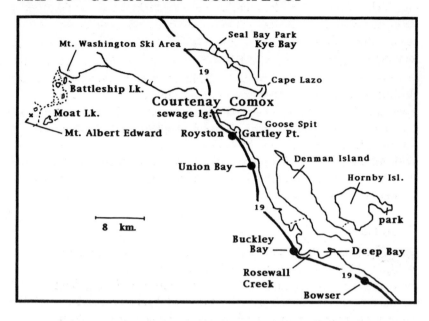

COURTENAY—COMOX LOOP

The Comox-Strathcona region includes one of the most important water bird habitats in British Columbia—the Baynes Sound / Comox Harbour complex. The Vancouver Island shoreline of Baynes Sound is comprised of estuaries, flooded fields, mud flats, salt marshes, a mixture of beach types, and subtidal zones. This variety of habitats attracts large numbers and a wide diversity of avifauna. Hundreds of thousands of sea ducks depend on the Baynes Sound/Comox Harbour area throughout the year, with winter showing the highest counts. Inland, traversing into the West Coast zone (that almost reaches the Straits of Georgia here), one ascends to subalpine elevations. A change in the character of the vegetation and consequently the avifauna is evident. The Mount Washington Ski Area is the most reliable area on Vancouver Island for finding all of the alpine species.

Victoria or Bowser to Deep Bay

We start our trip in the northern outskirts of Victoria at the Town and Country Shopping Plaza where Douglas Street veers sharply left to become Highway 1. It is a (212 km.), 3 to 3½ hour drive from Victoria to Courtenay, taking the new Nanaimo by-pass and new 4-lane highway northwards from Parksville. This highway can be taken as far as Campbell River if you wish to by-pass the congestion along the coast.. Alternatively, we can start the loop at Bowser which is 173 kilometers from Victoria or 31 kilometers north of Parksville.

(00.0 km.) A good place to start a birding tour of the region is at Deep Bay. Turn right off Highway 19 onto Gainsburg Road (3.8 km.) north of Bowser at the sign for Deep Bay. Continue on Gainsburg Road keeping left at the railway tracks. After driving (1.6 km.) (5.4 km.) you will see a Bald Eagle nest on the left in a lone dead tree very close to the road. After (0.3 km.) (5.7 km.) turn right onto Burne Road, then left onto Deep Bay Drive (0.1 km.) (5.8 km.). Park at the terminus below the lighthouse (1.0 km.) (6.8 km.).

Deep Bay

During the winter, in the channel between the spit and Denman Island, thousands of Western Grebe will be seen. There are large concentrations of Greater Scaup, Surf Scoter, White-winged Scoter and Black Scoter. The Surf and White-winged are commonly seen into the summer months. Pacific Loon, Common Loon, Common Murre, Marbled Murrelet and Pigeon Guillemot are abundant in winter and may be seen in summer. Proceed to the north end of the spit and scan for the Oldsquaw. At Deep Bay Harbour, tucked in on the opposite side of the spit, it is not unusual to see six species of gull; an occasional immature Herring Gull is found through summer. The rocky beach is favoured by numerous shorebirds. Prominent are wintering Black-bellied Plover and Black Turnstone. The Black Oystercatcher is an uncommon resident but Surfbird may be observed during migration. Parasitic Jaeger may pass through, seen harrasing the Common Tern when they are present during the fall. Long-tailed Jaeger and Pomarine Jaeger are rare but possible. Bald Eagle are ever present.

Pelagic Cormorant and Double-crested Cormorant, Great Blue Heron, Bufflehead and Belted Kingfisher are common in the harbour. Among the abundant American Wigeon, a Eurasian Wigeon makes an occasional appearance.

A variety of residential songbirds add more interest. The House Finch and Rufous Hummingbird brighten a dull day. In spring and summer Violet-green Swallow, Barn Swallow, Northern Rough-winged Swallow and American Goldfinch are commonly seen.

Return back along your route to the railway tracks and turn left onto Kopina Drive (2.7 km.) (9.5 km.), right onto Longview Road (0.1 km.) (9.6 km.) then left at Seaview Drive (0.1 km.) (9.7 km.). Seaview Drive changes name to Shoreline Drive. Proceed along Shoreline Drive and park on the left at (0.9 km.) (10.6 km.). From here there is a clear view across the channel to the Chrome Island lighthouse off the south end of Denman Island. Brandt's Cormorant roost here during the winter months. Large concentrations of Red-necked Grebe, Horned Grebe, and the occasional Eared Grebe frequent the channel with Common Merganser and Red-breasted Merganser in winter. In the typical lowland second-growth mixed forest on the opposite side of the road are Swainson's Thrush, Yellow-rumped Warbler, Western Tanager and the other species associated with this habitat.

Deep Bay to Rosewall Creek Park

Retrace your route back to Highway 19, turning right (00.0 km.). After driving (5.1 km.) turn right onto Berray Road for Rosewall Creek Park.

Rosewall Creek Park

This is a quiet road running through a lovely growth of mainly deciduous mixed woods. The trees are tall with sunlight dappled wildflowers at their bases and Rosewall Creek flows nearby. Heard, if not seen, will be Hammond's Flycatcher, Pacific-slope Flycatcher, Western Wood-Pewee (uncommon), Chestnut-backed Chickadee, Bewick's Wren, Winter Wren, Golden-crowned Kinglet, Swainson's Thrush, American Robin, Cassin's Vireo, Warbling Vireo, Red-eyed Vireo, Orange-crowned Warbler, Yellow Warbler, Black-throated Gray Warbler, Townsend's Warbler, MacGillivray's Warbler and Wilson's Warbler. From the depths of the woods the drumming of a Hairy Woodpecker is often heard.

Continue along Berray Road and turn nght onto Wavell Road (1.3 km.) (6.4 km.) and park at its terminus (0.3 km.) (6.7 km.). Look over the fields for Red-tailed Hawk. There is a record of the vagrant Swainson's Hawk. Check offshore for sea ducks, loons and alcids in season. The shoreline and small tidal area harbour migrating shorebirds. Bald Eagle are common.

Of interest to those who have the better part of a day to spend, would be to walk in a southerly direction along the shore to the Cook Creek Estuary but it is rough going on the uneven terrain. The salt marsh at the mouth of the creek is a favourite place for shorebirds. In late summer, Osprey and Merlin, and overhead, Common Nighthawk frequent the area.

Return to Highway 19 and park. Walk over the Rosewall Creek bridge. Step off on the right and walk under the bridge to the opposite side of the road to a trail along the river, a pleasant stroll on a hot day. Bird life is scarce in the deep, cool woods but an American Dipper is often seen along the stream.

Rosewall Creek Park to Ship's Point Road

Continue right on Highway 19 (00.0 km.). At Waterloo Creek (2.8 km.) or (11.7 km.) north of Bowser, park just across the bridge. Gas and refreshments are available at the Pacific Village Resort. Wander down to the mouth of the creek for seasonal sightings of Black Turnstone, Greater Yellowlegs and Dunlin. Red-breasted Sapsucker frequent the adjacent woods.

Ship's Point Road

Continue north along Highway 19, turning right onto Ship's Point Road (2.5 km.) (5.3 km.) and proceed to Tozer Road. Turn left and park (1.2 km.) (6.5 km.). Across the road is a Fish and Wildlife Management area. Included among the species of shorebirds attracted to this tidal marsh are transient Semipalmated Plover, Greater Yellowlegs, Lesser Yellowlegs, Solitary Sandpiper, Western Sandpiper, Least Sandpiper, Semipalmated Sandpiper, Pectoral Sandpiper, Baird's Sandpiper, Short-billed Dowitcher and Long-billed Dowitcher. Continue along Tozer Road and park at its terminus (1.4 km.) (7.9 km.). Walk to the right and follow the dike road through the yellow gate. On the bay are a variety of puddle ducks. Common Loon, Pacific Loon, Red-throated Loon, Pigeon Guillemot and Marbled Murrelet occur offshore. Mew Gull, Herring Gull, Thayer's Gull, California Gull (uncommon) and Bonaparte's Gull are found in season. Check the wet fields for Common Snipe and migrant shorebirds. Along the walkway look for Northern Shrike. A resident Barred Owl may be heard in the adjacent woods.

Ship's Point to Buckley Bay, Hornby & Denman Islands

Return to Highway 19, turning right (00.0 km.). At Buckley Bay (4.9 km.) or (19.1 km.) from Bowser you may board the ferry for the 15 minute crossing to Denman Island. There is excellent fall and winter birding at Henry Bay and Longbeak Point where there is an assembly of shorebirds. The accidental Snowy Plover was recorded here on May 28, 1972. Make this trip when the tide is low and be prepared for a long walk. At the opposite end of the island a woodland track leads to Boyle's Point which overlooks the picturesque Chrome Island lighthouse where Brandt's Cormorant roost.

Do not neglect a visit to the enchanting Helliwell Park on Hornby Island, a short ferry ride from Denman. You may roam through a forest of mature Douglas-fir, arbutus, and Garry oak to the rocky headlands. High cliffs support a nesting colony of Pelagic Cormorant and make good vantage points for observation of seabirds. Open grassy areas dotted with clusters of shrubs and small trees provide habitat for open country species.

To find your way around both of these small islands, call in at the General Store up the hill from the Denman Island ferry landing.

Buckley Bay to Royston

On returning to Vancouver Island, continue north on Highway 19 (00.0 km.). Between Buckley Bay and Union Bay the highway borders the shoreline. A rest stop at (3.1 km.) or (22.2 km.) from Bowser is found on the right. The rest stop provides a good site for open water viewing. Among the numerous waterfowl in the channel are Black Scoter. The Eared Grebe has been recorded, irregular this far north.

Royston

Continue along Highway 19 to Royston, turning right onto Gartley Road (6.9 km.) (14.0 km.) or (36.2 km.) from Bowser. A left turn just before the beach will take you to Gartley Point (0.8 km.) (14.8 km.). Old pilings in the channel are favourite perches for Double-crested Cormorant and Pelagic Cormorant. The beach is frequently covered with gulls. In the vicinity will be a Belted Kingfisher. The adjacent shrubbery and a small grove of trees afford habitat for Sharp-shinned Hawk, California Quail (uncommon), Band-tailed Pigeon, Rufous Hummingbird, Downy Woodpecker, Northern Flicker, Pacific-slope Flycatcher, Olive-sided Flycatcher, Bushtit, Bewick's Wren, Winter Wren, Swainson's Thrush, Cedar Waxwing, Warbling Vireo, Orange-crowned Warbler, Yellow-rumped Warbler, MacGillivray's Warbler, House Finch and Purple Finch. A King Eider wintered here recently.

Return to Highway 19, turning right (00.0 km.). After driving

(0.6 km.) turn right onto Carey Place and park at the turnaround (0.2 km.) (0.8 km.). A walk along the edge of the river to the estuary is often productive. A pair of Bullock's Oriole have nested in the area. Past the trees the landscape opens, the ground is covered with a tangle of sedges and grasses and debris left over from high tides and winter storms. If you are lucky, you may see Northern Harrier or Merlin.

Back at the highway (0.2 km.) (1.0 km.) turn right, then right again onto Hayward Avenue (0.2 km.) (1.2 km.) which leads down to the waterfront. Turn left onto Marine Drive (0.1 km.) (1.3 km.). In the fall and winter you will be able to observe Common Loon, Pacific Loon, Red-throated Loon, and various dabbling and sea ducks. Prominent among the dabblers are Northern Pintail. Diving ducks include Common Goldeneye, Barrow's Goldeneye, Canvasback (uncommon), Greater Scaup, Lesser Scaup (uncommon), Bufflehead, Common Merganser and Red-breasted Merganser. In March and April hundreds of Brant use the waterfront as a stopover on their north-ward migration. Common Tern are fall migrants. Gulls, mainly Glaucous-winged Gull, line the full-length of the pier. Others usually found in the vicinity include Rufous Hummingbird, Violet-green Swallow, Barn Swallow, Northern Rough-winged Swallow, Swainson's Thrush, Cedar Waxwing, Yellow Warbler, Chipping Sparrow, Savannah Sparrow, White-crowned Sparrow and Evening Grosbeak.

Royston to Cumberland

It you wish to make a side trip to historic Cumberland, turn left off Marine Drive onto Royston Road. Cumberland is (7.5 km.). When you arrive in Cumberland turn left onto Sutton Road at the sign for Comox Lake and continue, turning left at the historic site marker (0.9 km.) (8.4 km.).

Cumberland

Here at the long abandoned China Town site is a fascinating wetland area complete with beaver ponds. Just below "Jumbo's Cabin", an old overgrown roadbed provides easy access to the marshes. You may walk to the west (right) or east along the shoulder of Sutton Road. Your tally will likely include Ruffed Grouse, Barred Owl, Northern Saw-whet Owl, Rufous Hummingbird, Belted Kingfisher, Red-breasted Sapsucker (may be common around the beaver ponds), Willow Flycatcher, Pacific-slope Flycatcher, Swainson's Thrush, Warbling Vireo, Orange-crowned Warbler, Yellow Warbler, Black-throated Gray Warbler,

MacGillivray's Warbler, Common Yellowthroat, Black-headed Grosbeak, Spotted Towhee, Song Sparrow, Red-winged Blackbird, Brown-headed Cowbird, Purple Finch, Red Crossbill and Pine Siskin. You may find a pair of Canada Geese nesting or hear a Pied-billed Grebe's cuckoo-like calls emitting from the marsh vegetation. Ring-necked Duck could be encountered.

Royston to Courtenay

Back at Royston on Marine Drive, veer left back onto Highway 19 (1.4 km.) (2.7 km.) and turn right. At Millard Road (2.4 km) (51 km.) turn right and park at the corner of Sandpiper Road (0.2 km.) (5.3 km.). This is one of a number of locations prefered by Trumpeter Swan. Over the years these birds have steadily increased in numbers.

At low tide, the mud flats provide habitat for a variety of shorebirds. Spaced out in mid-channel one can often see 20 to 30 Great Blue Heron. There are large concentrations of Mallard and American Wigeon and the odd Eurasian Wigeon among them. The Snow Goose is an uncommon transient. Canada Geese are common residents. Bonaparte's Gull are seen in good numbers in May and June as well as in the usual migration frame. Resident song birds in the area include Chestnut-backed Chickadee, Red-breasted Nuthatch, Bushtit, Golden-crowned Kinglet, Varied Thrush, Spotted Towhee, Song Sparrow, Dark-eyed Junco, Purple Finch and House Finch. Populations fluctuate according to season.

Courtenay

Return to Highway 19, turning right (0.1 km.) (5.4 km.). Our next stop is Courtenay. Turn right at Mansfield Drive opposite the Driftwood Mall (1.3 km.) (6.7 km.). There are some good sites from which to observe the bird life, especially shorebirds at the mouth of the Courtenay river and surrounding beach.

Continue on Mansfield Drive veering left back to Highway 19 (0.4 km.) (7.4 km.) and turn right. At the traffic lights on 17th Avenue, turn right over the bridge for the continuation of Highway 19 (0.8 km.) (8.2 km.). Once over the bridge, turn right onto Dyke Road (00.0 km.) or left for Mount Washington Ski Area or Puntledge Park (0.4 km.) (8.6 km.).

Those wishing to visit Puntledge Park, continue along Highway 19 turning left onto Comox Road (0.5 km.) (9.1 km.). Drive an additional (0.3 km.) (9.4 km.) turning right onto the Old Island Highway and park in the parking lot on the left side of the highway (0.1 km.) (9.5 km.). Puntledge Park is a delightful place in the city of Courtenay where one can picnic beside the Puntledge River and perhaps see an American Dipper or a Green Heron (both uncommon). Wander the paths through the woods—Bushtit, Bewick's Wren and Chestnut-backed Chickadee will greet you. Downy Woodpecker and Brown Creeper should not be missed. Watch for Black Swift overhead. Resident Evening Grosbeak are erratic, but possible.

Those wishing to visit the Mount Washington Ski Area continue on Highway 19, turning left from the 17th Avenue bridge (00.0 km.) to the second set of traffic lights and proceed straight ahead on Headquarters Road (1.7 km.). There is a large sign designating the direction to the ski area at this corner. Continue on Headquarters Road for an additional (1.7 km.) (3.4 km.), turning left onto Piercy Road (Dove Creek Road). For continuation of directions, see page 127 and reverse.

Back on our loop, turn right onto Dyke Road (00.0 km.). At (1.2 km.) park at the viewing stand past the mill on the right. Across the road is the Dyke Slough and acres of rich farmlands. Watch for traffic!

Mansfield-Dyke Slough

For birders, the Mansfield-Dyke section is perhaps the most exciting area in the region. This is where you are most likely to see the rarities and accidentals. The following have been recorded: Leach's Storm-Petrel, Cattle Egret, Great Egret, Gyrfalcon, Marbled Godwit, Black-necked Stilt, Willet, Ruff, Sharp-tailed Sandpiper and Yellow-headed Blackbird.

Trumpeter Swan are the highlight in the winter, they are seen by the hundreds spread over the farmlands. A few Tundra Swan will be noted especially during migration. An unconfirmed Whooper Swan was seen in November 1998 and another confirmed record in the region a few years earlier during August. The August record would most likely be an escapee. Resident gaggles of Canada Geese come and go, while Greater White-fronted Goose and Snow Goose are uncommon transients. Watch for Peregrine Falcon hunting the fields where migrant American Pipit are found during the fall months. Brewer's Blackbird, Red-winged Blackbird, American Goldfinch and Savannah Sparrow frequent the fields and migrant Lincoln's Sparrow will be found in moist brushy and grass areas in migration.

From the viewing stand, scope the mud flats for shorebirds. The best time is on an incoming tide. Killdeer are common residents. The usual species are present with Greater Yellowlegs, Lesser Yellowlegs, Solitary Sandpiper, Spotted Sandpiper, Semipalmated Sandpiper, Western Sandpiper, Least Sandpiper, Baird's Sandpiper, Pectoral Sandpiper, Sanderling, Dunlin, Short-billed Dowitcher and Long-billed Dowitcher. Other less common species of shorebird are to be expected. Check the lombardy poplars next to the viewing stand for a pair of Bullock's Oriole that have nested.

At the slough you will find summering Blue-winged Teal and Cinnamon Teal. Mallard are resident. In the winter months look for Green-winged Teal, Northern Pintail, Northern Shoveler, Gadwall (rare), Ruddy Duck (sporadic) and American Coot. The population of Green Heron is slowly increasing and is now an uncommon summer resident. Wilson's Phalarope are rare migrants. Among the passerines are Violet-green Swallow, Northern Rough-winged Swallow, Barn Swallow, Bank Swallow (rare migrant), Cedar Waxwing, European Starling, Yellow Warbler, Common Yellowthroat, Red-winged Blackbird, Brown-headed Cowbird, Purple Finch and House Finch. This is the only likely site you will find Marsh Wren.

The tall sitka spruces neighbouring the sawmill are favourite look-outs for Bald Eagle. In summer look for Turkey Vulture which often float overhead on dihedral wings, circling high over the fields with just the odd tilting movement of their wings.

Dyke Slough to Comox and Goose Spit

Turn right and continue along Dyke Road towards Comox. Dyke Road will change name to Comox Avenue. There are several places where you may pull off the road to scope the flats. At (2.4 km.) check through the gulls for Ring-billed Gull in the summer months (not uncommon) and for summering immature Herring Gull. After (1.8 km.) (4.2 km.) turn right past the hospital onto Beach Avenue and drive to its terminus and park (0.6 km.) (4.8 km.). This is a good place to look for migrant Whimbrel in the spring. Bewick's Wren and House Finch are present.

Return to Comox Avenue (0.6 km.) (5.4 km.) and turn right. At Pritchard Street follow the sign for Goose Spit and turn left (1.4 km.) (6.8 km.), then right onto Balmoral (0.3 km.) (7.1 km.) where there is another sign for the spit. At the three-way stop go straight ahead onto Hawkins Road (0.6 km.) (7.7 km.) and proceed to Goose Spit and park (1.1 km.) (8.8 km.). Watch for California Quail (uncommon) in the residential area en route to the spit.

Goose Spit

In the winter the bay shelters large populations of bay and sea ducks with Common Loon, Pacific Loon, Surf Scoter, Marbled Murrelet and Pigeon Guillemot seen through into summer. Flocks of over a thousand Brant stop over in spring migration. Flocks of summering Bonaparte's Gull will be encountered. Osprey are often seen fishing. Shorebirding is good on the mudflats and outer shore. Snowy Owl may be seen in winters of invasions.

Goose Spit to Lazo Marsh

Return to the three-way stop, turning right onto Lazo Road (1.1 km.) (9.9 km.) and right onto Lazo again (0.1 km.) (10.0 km.). After (0.8 km.) (10.8 km.) Lazo makes a left. Continue along Lazo Road, turning left onto an old paved road section after driving (1.4 km.) (12.2 km.). The path for Lazo Marsh is found on the left of this old road. Soras are found in the marsh. Try "owling" on a calm evening, a Western Screech-Owl or Northern Saw-whet Owl may respond to your taped calls. Red-breasted Sapsucker frequent the woods. Yellow Warbler and Common Yellowthroat sing from the edges of the marsh. In the typical lowland mixed second-growth forest are birds of this habitat including Hutton's Vireo.

Lazo Marsh to Pt. Holmes, Comox Airport & Kye Bay

Continue on Lazo Road. As you pass Brent Road on the left look for the Osprey nest clearly visible above the road. After (1.8 km.) (14.0 km.) pull off next to the boat launching ramp at Point Holmes. Many thousands of gulls line the beach when the herring are spawning. Most are Glaucous-winged Gull, Mew Gull and Thayer's Gull with lesser numbers of Ring-billed Gull and Herring Gull. Throughout the year you will see Double-crested Cormorant and Pelagic Cormorant perching on big boulders offshore. Expected are Common Loon Pacific Loon, Surf Scoter, White-winged Scoter, Black Scoter and Harlequin Duck. Look on tidelines well-offshore during the fall for Red-necked Phalarope (uncommon) and Red Phalarope (rare).

Continue on Lazo Road to Kye Bay Road and turn right (0.5 km.) (14.5 km.). Check the short-grass runways of the Comox Airport for migrating American Pipit and Horned Lark. Horned Lark once breed here but have not done so since 1970. Buff-breasted Sandpiper, American Golden-Plover and Pacific Golden-Plover should be looked for. Two Buff-breasted Sandpiper were recorded on August 21, 1973. Other "uplands" and open-country rarities should be expected. Yellow-headed Blackbird has been recorded. Along the perimeter fence are Savannah Sparrow, Brewer's Blackbird and House Finch.

Continue along Kye Bay Road and park at the terminus at Kye Bay (2.0 km.) (16.5 km.). The small bay is fair for shorebirds. A Curlew Sandpiper was seen here on July 11, 1981 and three days later was seen at Victoria.

Kye Bay to Powell River Ferry Terminal

Return to Lazo Road (1.9 km.) (18.4 km.) and turn right. Lazo changes its name to Knight Road. Proceed along Knight Road for (1.7 km.) (20.1 km.). On your left you will see some rather weary looking buildings with the name "Comox Valley Produce". During the winter the whole area is under water and is particularly attractive to Trumpeter Swan, Mallard and American Wigeon. Hundreds of each of these species can be observed from the roadside.

Continue along Knight Road. After driving (2.0 km.) (22.1 km.) there are Willow Flycatcher in the scrubby lots. Red-eyed Vireo may be found in the deciduous patches.

After (0.3 km.) (22.4 km.) turn right onto Little River Road, passing the Air Base on your right. Follow the winding road to Wilkinson Road (3.9 km.) (26.3 km.) and turn left, then right onto Singing Sands Road (0.3 km.) (26.6 km.). Park at the terminus (0.6 km.) (27.2 km.). This is an excellent site from which to view sea ducks. The predominant species is the Oldsquaw. Among others you will find are Greater Scaup, Common Goldeneye and Bufflehead.

Return to Wilkinson Road (0.5 km.) (27.7 km.) and turn right. At Ellenor Road (0.8 km.) (28.5 km.) turn right for the Powell River Ferry Terminal (0.3 km.) (28.8 km.). Time your arrival so as to coincide with the ferry schedule. On cold winter days, scope the waterfowl from the comfort of your car. Check for shorebirds.

Powell River Ferry Terminal to Seal Bay Nature Park

Retrace your route back along Ellenor Road, turning sharply right onto Anderson Road (1.6 km.) (30.4 km.) which changes name to Waveland Road. After (3.8 km.) (34.2 km.) turn left from Waveland onto Bates Road. After (1.3 km.) (35.5 km.) pull over into the Seal Bay Nature Park's parking lot where there is a map of the trails.

Seal Bay Nature Park

The park is comprised of 325 acres of typical lowland mixed second-growth forest. Take a stroll around the swamp trail where you will find Hairy Woodpecker, Olive-sided Flycatcher, Willow Flycatcher, Hammond's Flycatcher, Pacific-slope Flycatcher, Steller's Jay, Chestnut-backed Chickadee, Bushtit, Red-breasted Nuthatch, Brown Creeper, Bewick's Wren, Winter Wren, Golden-crowned Kinglet, Cassin's Vireo, Hutton's Vireo, Yellow Warbler, Yellow-rumped Warbler, Black-throated Gray Warbler, Townsend's Warbler, MacGillivray's Warbler, Wilson's Warbler, Common Yellowthroat, Spotted Towhee, Western Tanager, Song Sparrow, Red-winged Blackbird, Purple Finch, Red Crossbill and Pine Siskin. The Red-breasted Sapsucker is seen occasionally and Three-toed Woodpecker has rarely come down from the sub-alpine to winter here.

Seal Bay Nature Park to Mount Washington Ski Area

Continue on Bates Road and turn left onto Coleman Road (3.5 km) (38.0 km.). At (39.6 km. and 40.7 km.) there are brushy areas with Willow Flycatcher. Look overhead for Black Swift, especially if a storm front is approaching. Continue on Coleman Road back to Highway 19 (1.5 km.) (42.2 km.).

From this junction you may continue north to Campbell River (35 km.) or turn left back to Courtenay (11 .9 km.).

You may also reach Mount Washington Ski Area by turning right onto Highway 19 (00.0 km.). At Merville Road (1.0 km.) turn left. After driving along Merville Road for (2.1 km.) (3.2 km.) continue straight ahead for Mount Washington Ski Area following the sign. After driving an additional (1.8 km.) (5.0 km.) turn left onto Fitzgerald Road following the sign for Paradise Meadows Park. After (0.6 km.) (5.6 km.) turn right onto Farnham Road. The road from here to the summit is excellent gravel. Watch for both Blue Grouse and Ruffed Grouse on the sides of the road en route.

After (6.9 km.) (12.5 km.) stop at the stop sign and proceed straight ahead for an additional 18.3 kilometers. From here you will quickly ascend into the East Coast zone and through it into the West Coast zone. After driving (7.3 km.) (19.8 km.) keep left (sign), then after (9.6 km.) (29.4 km.) keep left—right leads to the ski lodges.

Mount Washington Ski Area

Park at the trail head (1.6 km.) (31.0 km.) where there is a sign Mt. Washington Cross Country. A complete map of the trails is displayed here. Draw a sketch with the place names before starting out. To reach the White-tailed Ptarmigan you must walk about 16 kilometers one-way! If you are in very good shape, and walk at a very quick pace, you can make it there and back in one day. You must start at daybreak, and with one hour to look for the ptarmigan, will be back at dusk. The Three-toed Woodpecker can be found by walking around the sub-alpine areas much closer to the parking area.

A tour of this region would not be complete without a visit to Paradise Meadows. The meadows are at an elevation of about 4,000 ft. Easy walking chip trails are found throughout. Each trail intersection has sign posts with the destinations and kilometers to each displayed. Here in the sub-alpine indications of the altitude are apparent in the characteristic species of trees and other vegetation. The best time to come is in August, but you may look for the woodpecker in the lower areas as early June.

Birders may find the area somewhat disappointing. Few birds will be seen on a single visit. With luck and patience you may record: Blue Grouse, Red-breasted Sapsucker and Three-toed Woodpecker (both of these species are rare), Hairy Woodpecker, Chestnut-backed Chickadee, Golden-crowned Kinglet, Hermit Thrush, Varied Thrush and Dark-eyed Junco. The Gray Jay is an ever present companion at this elevation.

Battleship Lake may be the best site to look for the Three-toed Woodpecker. It has nested in the area of the washrooms. You will be very fortunate to find this rarest of the Vancouver Island residents. Battleship Lake is an easy one-hour hike. From the parking lot, keep right at the first fork to Paradise Meadows. At the second fork, follow the sign to the left and on to the lake (1.7 km.) away. En route, keep right at the next fork where another sign points the way. At the south end of the lake you will find a camping area and the washrooms. The trail continues around to the west side of the lake.

The most likely place to see White-tailed Ptarmigan on Vancouver Island is on the rocky slopes to the summit of Mount Albert Edward at 6,868 ft. The ptarmigan should not be missed if you come in August when the parent birds are protecting their chicks and thus less secretive. American Pipit and Gray-crowned Rosy Finch are possible but are not to be expected. Look especially around the remaining snow patches where the rosy finch may be found picking insects from the ice.

To reach Mount Albert Edward, follow the trail to Hair Trigger Lake (6.9 km.) keeping right at the trails to Paradise Meadows and Battleship Lake. En route, keep right at the fork that leads to the south shore of Battleship Lake and right at the next junction. From Hair Trigger Lake it is approximately (9.0 km.) to the alpine ridges. Keep left at the junction for Circlet Lake and right at the junction for Moat Lake. The walk to this point will have been very easy. In front of you is a very steep climb to the ridge, which is now close. A hinterland of snow-spattered, flower-strewn, and lichen-dominated alpine meadows greet you as soon as you reach the ridge. The views are magnificent! Above treeline start looking for the ptarmigan. The ptarmigan can be hard to see, relying on their camouflage and you may easily walk right past them as their mottled summer plumage will make them close to invisible. Search the rocky rubble slopes towards the serrated peak of Mount Albert Edward, etched against the cerulean sky, or sit still and watch for movement.

(00.0 km.) To reach downtown Courtenay, return back to the stop sign (18.3 km.). Proceed ahead for an additional (1.1 km.) (19.4 km.), turning right onto Dove Creek Road where there is a sign for Courtenay. After (2.7 km.) (22.1 km.) you will reach pavement. Dove Creek Road makes a sharp left (24.5 km) and then a sharp right (25.0 km). After (1.5 km.) (26.5 km.) Dove Creek changes name to Condensory Road. Proceed straight ahead. After an additional (1.6 km.) (28.1 km) you may continue ahead for Courtenay or turn left onto Piercy Road. We will turn onto Piercy Road. After (0.8 km.) (28.9 km.) stop and turn right onto Dove Creek Road (Piercy Road). After (1.0 km.) (29.9 km.) turn right onto Headquarters Road back into Courtenay. After (1.7 km.) (31.6 km.) you will rejoin Highway 19. Reverse these directions from this point it you are going up to the ski area from Courtenay.

To report rarities while in the area, contact the Victoria Rare Bird Alert (250) 592-3381.

MAP 17—CAMPBELL RIVER LOOP

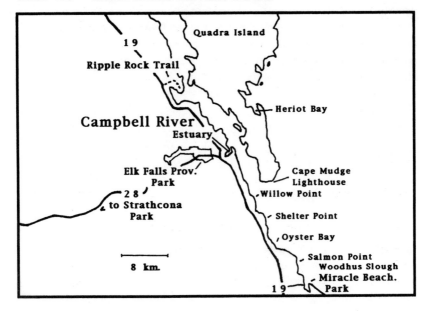

CAMPBELL RIVER LOOP

Campbell River lies at the extreme northern parameter of the Southeast Coastal Lowlands. Many of the Southeast Coastal Lowland "specialties" are much less common—or absent—as is the case with the California Quail. Campbell River is 240 kilometers north of Victoria and is a 4 to $4\frac{1}{2}$ hour drive, using the freeway.

Courtenay to Miracle Beach Park

We start this loop from the 17th Avenue bndge in downtown Courtenay making a left turn onto Highway 19 North (00.0 km.). Drive north on Highway 19 turning right onto Miracle Beach Road (22.8 km.) or (24.2 km.) south of Campbell River.

Miracle Beach Park

There are signs for Miracle Beach Park. Continue on to the park (25.6 km.) keeping left for the nature house or right for camping. There are 193 campsites surrounded by typical lowland mixed second-growth forest and there are two kms. of trails that include beautiful beaches.

Pileated Woodpecker are especially numerous and easy to find. Western Screech-Owl and Northern Saw-whet Owl will be found "owling" around the campsites. Caspian Tern (erratic) are often seen on the beaches. In the forests are the species common to this habitat including Red-breasted Sapsucker (uncommon), Hairy Woodpecker, Hammond's Flycatcher, Pacific-slope Flycatcher, Chestnut-backed Chickadee, Red-breasted Nuthatch, Brown Creeper, Winter Wren, Golden-crowned Kinglet, Swainson's Thrush, American Robin, Cassin's Vireo, Warbling Vireo, Hutton's Vireo, Red-eyed Vireo, Orange-crowned Warbler, Yellow-rumped Warbler, Townsend's Warbler, MacGillivray's Warbler, Spotted Towhee, Western Tanager, Song Sparrow, Purple Finch, Red Crossbill and Pine Siskin. Two rarities that have been recorded here are Northern Mockingbird and Nashville Warbler.

Miracle Beach Park to Woodhus Slough

Return to Highway 19 and turn right (00.0 km.). At (4.2 km.) turn right onto Salmon Point Road and park at the restaurant on the very aesthetic sandy point (4.9 km.). Walk back along the road 50 yards, taking the public trail south through the sand-dune habitat to a grassy marsh of Woodhus Slough. Sora and Virginia Rail inhabit the marsh in summer. Western Meadowlark may be found during the winter months. Yellow Warbler, Common Yellowthroat and Red-winged Blackbird are common summer residents with rare records of Marsh Wren. Bewick's Wren frequent the brushy patches. The area is especially interesting during migration when such rarities as Long-tailed Jaeger, Snowy Owl, Black-billed Magpie, Mountain Bluebird and Yellow-headed Blackbird have been recorded.

Woodhus Slough to Shelter Point and Willow Point

Return to Highway 19 and turn right (5.6 km.). At (12.8 km.) pull off at the Shelter Point-Oyster Bay shoreline. This area is excellent in the fall for migrating seabirds including Parasitic Jaeger, Common Tern and Red-necked Phalarope. Among the expected waterbirds one will find Red-throated Loon, Pacific Loon, Common Loon, Horned Grebe, Red-necked Grebe, Western Grebe (thousands of Western Grebe pause in Oyster Bay during migration), Double-crested Cormorant, Pelagic Cormorant, Great Blue Heron, Brant (spring migration-occasionally in summer), Greater Scaup, Harlequin Duck, Surf Scoter (mainly non-breeders during summer), White-winged Scoter, Black Scoter, Common Goldeneye, Bufflehead, Common Merganser and

Red-breasted Merganser. Bald Eagle are ever present. Marbled Murrelet, Common Murre and Pigeon Guillemot are resident.

Continue along Highway 19 and pull off at Willow Point (16.5 km.). You will find the birding similar to Shelter Point. Gulls are often more numerous with thousands of migrating Bonaparte's Gull, Mew Gull, California Gull, Herring Gull (a few), Thayer's Gull and Glaucous-winged Gull in season.

Willow Point to Campbell River / Quadra Island

Proceed to downtown Campbell River and turn at the sign for Highway 19 and for the Quadra Island Ferry (24.0 km.).

Quadra Island

For those wishing to take a trip to this lovely island, board the ferry for the short trip. You will land at Quathiaski cove. Take Cape Mudge and Lighthouse Roads south to the Cape Mudge Lighthouse (9.0 km.). From the lighthouse there are spectacular views of Discovery Passage. In winter, scan the passage for thousands of loons, commorants (including Brandt's), Common Murre, Marbled Murrelet and Pigeon Guillemot. Several species of pelagic birds have been seen from this vantage point including Sooty Shearwater and Black-legged Kittiwake.

Return to Quathiaski Cove and continue north to Heriot Bay via West and Heriot Bay Roads (approx. 6.4 km.) and proceed east to Drew Harbour and Rebecca Spit Park (9.6 km.). At this site during winter are many sea ducks including White-winged Scoter, Harlequin Duck and Barrow's Goldeneye. Large numbers of Pacific Loons also winter in the area.

Continue back through Heriot Bay. Western Bluebird (rare) are possible in the old orchards. Virginia Rail inhabit local marshes during summer. A drive north to Granite Bay (16.0 km.) via West, Cramer, and Granite Bay Roads should produce Turkey Vulture, which nest in the immediate vicinity, and excellent views of migrant hawks.

Campbell River Estuary

Back on Vancouver Island we continue our loop as we proceed north on Highway 19. At (25.0 km.) turn right onto Spit Road for the Campbell River Estuary (00.0 km.). Follow the Okanagan Helicopter signs. This area is good for resident and migrating species due to the varied habitats, a large estuary, salt and fresh water marshes, a mixture of beach types, and subtidal zones. Peregrine Falcon and Snowy Owl are present most winters.

Wintering species such as Pied-billed Grebe (resident) and American Coot are to be expected. The usual species in the marshy brush are Rufous Hummingbird, Warbling Vireo, Yellow Warbler, Common Yellowthroat, Cedar Waxwing and Purple Finch. Check the cattail marsh (0.5 km.) down the road for Virginia Rail. At (1.8 km.) check offshore for the usual sea ducks and Pacific Loon, Marbled Murrelet, Common Murre and Pigeon Guillemot. At (2.3 km.) look the estuary over for shorebirds. Many non-breeding Bonaparte's Gull are found summering through May and June, as well as during the usual migration periods. Although unrecorded, the Little Gull should be looked for. Caspian Tern (uncommon) are seen errati-cally. Bald Eagle are ever present. Rarities recorded here include: Eared Grebe, Cattle Egret, Snow Goose (uncommon), Garganey, Canvasback, Black-legged Kittiwake, Mourning Dove, Purple Martin, Bushtit (north-ern limits) and Northern Mockingbird.

Campbell River Estuary to Elk Falls Park

Return to Highway 19 and turn right. After driving (1.9 km.) you will come to a major intersection. You can turn right for the continuation of Highway 19 North for a drive into the northeastern sector of Vancouver Island, or the ferry at Port Hardy or for a hike at Cape Scott (285 km.). Highway 28 begins from this point—continue straight ahead. Our loop will continue from this junction—straight ahead onto Highway 28 (00.0 km.). At (1.4 km.) turn left into the Quinsam Campsite of Elk Falls Provincial Park.

Elk Falls Provincial Park

There are 121 campsites settled in typical lowland mixed sec-ond-growth forest. Among the usual species in this habitat are Pileated Woodpecker, Hairy Woodpecker, Hammond's Fly-catcher, Pacific-slope Flycatcher, Chestnut-backed Chickadee, Red-breasted Nuthatch, Brown Creeper, Winter Wren, Golden-crowned Kinglet, Swainson's Thrush, American Robin, Cassin's Vireo, Warbling Vireo, Hutton's Vireo, Yellow Warbler, Townsend's Warbler, Western Tanager, Song Sparrow and the uncommon Black-headed Grosbeak. The grosbeak may be found along the river trail. American Dipper inhabit Quinsam and Campbell River rapids with the odd Ring-necked Duck in quiet pools.

Elk Falls Park to Strathcona Provincial Park

For those wishing to do some strenuous hiking, continue on Highway 28 to Strathcona Provincial Park. Starting the trip from Elk Falls Provincial Park at (00.0 km.), turn left. Highway 28 has many sharp curves and follows the shorelines of both Upper Campbell and Buttle Lakes. Here you will follow a long finger of the East Coast bio-geoclimatic zone deep into the West Coast zone along Buttle Lake. Birds typical of this zone will be found along the lakeshore including Hammond's Flycatcher (abundant) and Western Tanager (uncommon).

At (38.8 km.) the Strathcona Park Lodge is found on the right.

Strathcona Provincial Park

There are several campsites and hiking trails that are marked with large signs. The best trail is the Flower Ridge Trail at (75.0 km.). The trail leads steeply up to alpine ridges. It is a 12 kms. return trip to the north end of the trail or 24 kms. to the south end (return) where the White-tailed Ptarmigan are found. It will take 4-5 hours to reach the north end where Three-toed Woodpecker (rare) may be found. There is a 4,000 ft. climb—not for the non-hiker! Gray Jay are common in the higher elevations. |At the parking lot and along the lower parts of the trail are Steller's Jay, Hairy Woodpecker, Hammond's Flycatcher, Olive-sided Flycatcher, Chestnut-backed Chickadee, Red-breasted Nuthatch (uncommon), Winter Wren, Golden-crowned Kinglet, Swainson's Thrush, Varied Thrush, American Robin, Warbling Vireo, Orange-crowned Warbler, Yellow-rumped Warbler, Townsend's Warbler, MacGillivray's Warbler, Spotted Towhee and Western Tanager (both uncommon) and Purple Finch.

Return to Campbell River.

MAP 18—NORTHEASTERN VANCOUVER ISLAND LOOP

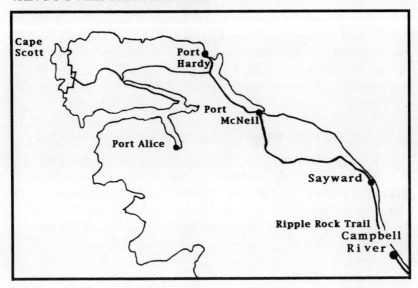

NORTHEASTERN VANCOUVER ISLAND

One of the most relaxing and scenic drives on Vancouver Island is along Highway 19 in the northeastern sector. The road is paved to Port Hardy where you may board the ferry to Prince Rupert. There are few sharp curves to slow progress or to stress the driver. Many uncrowded rest stops in a range of habitats from slash through lovely lakesides, mixed woodlands, and coniferous woods are available to find the limited variety of species in this region. As you approach the lowlands at Port McNeill through Port Hardy you will enter the West Coast bio-geoclimatic zone (and consequently leaving East Coast avifauna) and will soon find Fox Sparrow and Hermit Thrush breeding alongside the highway.

The more common species to expect in their proper habitats and zones along the length of Highway 19 are: Bald Eagle, Red-tailed Hawk, Blue Grouse, Ruffed Grouse, Band-tailed Pigeon, Western Screech-Owl, Northern Pygmy-Owl, Rufous Hummingbird, Hairy Woodpecker, Northern Flicker, Olive-sided Flycatcher, Hammond's Flycatcher, Northern Rough-winged Swallow, Steller's Jay, Northwestern Crow, Common Raven, Chestnut-backed

Chickadee, Winter Wren, Golden-crowned Kinglet, Ruby-crowned Kinglet (uncommon summer resident), Swainson's Thrush, Varied Thrush, American Robin, Cedar Waxwing, Warbling Vireo, Hutton's Vireo, Orange-crowned Warbler, Yellow Warbler (very local), Yellow-rumped Warbler, Townsend's Warbler, MacGillivray's Warbler, Wilson's Warbler, Common Yellowthroat (local), Spotted Towhee (slashes), Western Tanager (uncommon), Song Sparrow, White-crowned Sparrow, Dark-eyed Junco, Brown-headed Cowbird, Purple Finch, Red Crossbill and Pine Siskin.

Campbell River to Ripple Rock Trail

From the junction of Highways 19 and 28, turn right onto Highway 19 North (00.0 km.). Settlements are few in this region, so keep your gas tank full! After driving (16.8 km.) there is a very inconspicuous brown trail parking sign on the right-hand side of the highway (look for three gray power generators on the left) for Ripple Rock Trail.

Ripple Rock Trail

The trail is eight kilometers in length (return) through prime mixed forest. The trail follows a powerline cut where the bird life is more varied. A few species to expect are Downy Woodpecker, Hairy Woodpecker, Hammond's Flycatcher, Swainson's Thrush, Varied Thrush, Warbling Vireo, Orange-crowned Warbler and Townsend's Warbler. Along the Menzies Creek Estuary you may be fortunate to find Marsh Wren in the fall. Many gulls and ducks use Menzies Bay for feeding and resting during migrations.

Ripple Rock Trail to Sayward and Salmon River Estuary

Proceed on Highway 19 North to the Sayward junction (45.0 km.) (61.8 km.), turning right for Sayward and the Salmon River Estuary (12.2 km.) (74.0 km.).

Sayward

Sayward lies in an isolated area of lowland agricultural lands, the northernmost habitat of its kind on Vancouver Island. Consequently, there are good numbers of Yellow Warbler and Common Yellowthroat in the available brushy bogs and Brewer's Blackbird and

Red-winged Blackbird in the bogs and farmlands. There are rare records of Black-headed Grosbeak and Bullock's Oriole, although breeding has not been proven. Spotted Towhee are common throughout the brushy margins. Birding along the many quiet farm roads as productive.

The Salmon River Estuary is excellent for migrating and wintering dabbling ducks and sea ducks and is the best habitat north of Comox Bay. There are many wintering Trumpeter Swan. The estuary harbours many species of migrant shorebird with Dunlin and Sanderling present most winters. To reach the estuary, turn right at Kelsey Way in "downtown" Sayward, across the Industrial Road (that is closed to public transport) onto a rough gravel road. You may also scope the flats from the main road at the mill. Check the sewage lagoons at the edge of the mill (the fenced area opposite the other (eastern) end of Kelsey Way), Sabine's Gull has been seen. There are plenty of swallows including Barn Swallow, Violet-green Swallow and Northern Rough-winged Swallow.

Sayward to Port Hardy and Port McNeill & Cape Scott

Return to Highway 19, turning right. Continue northward stopping at the numerous rest stops along the way. At Port McNeill (129.0 km.) (191.0 km.) you will enter the West Coast bio-geoclimatic zone. Between Port McNeill and Port Hardy (36.0 km.) (227.0 km.) listen for the sweet song of the Fox Sparrow along the brushy margins of the road or at stream crossings. Hermit Thrush sing from the denser stands of conifers where the ground and many of the trees are completely cushioned in spongy mosses. These sombre forests are made more mystical by the ethereal piercing notes of Varied Thrush.

At Port Hardy you will find all amenities, be sure to gas-up for the return trip. It you are an ardent hiker, continue on the gravel road just south of Port Hardy for Cape Scott Park an additional (58.0 km.). The road is signed for the park and Holberg and Winter Harbour. Use the West Coast column 1 of the checklist for this region.

MAY 2000

392 Species

The following is a complete checklist of the birds of Vancouver Island as of May 2000; a total of 392 (which includes 4 extripated and 8 introduced species)—plus 25 hypotheticals and 1 uncountable species (Wild Turkey). A quick inspection of the following bar-graphs (along with the colour-coded range maps in the National Geographic's *Field Guide to the Birds of North America* which display the seasonal distribution of birds) will furnish you with complete information on the seasonal occurrence and relative abundance of Vancouver Island's avifauna. Order of birds follows the National Geographic's *Field Guide to the Birds of North America*.

For bar graph and status symbol explanations, please see page 148.

SPECIES	1	2	3	CALENDAR J F M A M J J A S O N D	√
LOONS					
☐ Common Loon*					
☐ Yellow-billed Loon	...	...	...		
☐ Pacific Loon					
☐ Red-throated Loon*					
GREBES					
☐ Western Grebe					
☐ Clark's Grebe	?	?	o ?	? o ? o ? ?	
☐ Red-necked Grebe*					
☐ Horned Grebe					
☐ Eared Grebe	o	o oo			
☐ Pied-billed Grebe*					
ALBATROSS					
☐ Short-tailed Albatross [A]	o o			o o	
☐ Black-footed Albatross			o		
☐ Laysan Albatross	..		o		
SHEARWATERS & PETRELS					
☐ Northern Fulmar		.. .	oo	.. .. .. — ..	
☐ Flesh-footed Shearwater	...				
☐ Sooty Shearwater		...l.	..	?	
☐ Short-tailed Shearwater	. . .		oo	•• •• ? •• •• ••	
☐ Pink-footed Shearwater				? ?	
☐ Buller's Shearwater	.	.		?	
☐ Black-vented Shearwater [R]	? •••			o ? o o	
☐ Mottled Petrel [R]	• •				
STORM-PETRELS					
☐ Leach's Storm-Petrel*	.., .	.., .	..	. . . .	
☐ Fork-tailed Storm-Petrel*			...	.. ..	
FRIGATEBIRD & TROPICBIRD					
☐ Magnificent Frigatebird [SR] ¥	??			? ? o ?	
☐ Red-tailed Tropicbird [remains]	o			o	
PELICANS					
☐ American White Pelican [A]			•••	. •• •• • • •• •	
☐ Brown Pelican [R]	..,	..,	oo	. .. .	
CORMORANTS					
☐ Double-crested Cormorant*					
☐ Brandt's Cormorant*					
☐ Pelagic Cormorant*					
BITTERNS & HERONS					
☐ American Bittern*	oo		...	.. ..	
☐ Black-crowned Night-Heron [R]				•• • • •• •• •• •• ••	

SPECIES	1	2	3	CALENDAR J F M A M J J A S O N D	√
☐ Green Heron*	...	...	IIII.	.. ..	
☐ Little Blue Heron [A]			o	o	
☐ Cattle Egret	. .	..	..	.. .. . —	
☐ Snowy Egret [A]	?			o o o o	
☐ Great Egret [R]	o		• ••	• .. • .. • .. • .. • ..	
☐ Great Blue Heron*	IIIII	IIIII	IIIII		
IBISES & CRANES					
☐ White-faced Ibis [A]	o oo		?	o o o o o o ? o o o	
☐ Sandhill Crane*	I.I	I.I.	I.I	.. .. .. — .. .. .. •	
WATERFOWL					
☐ Tundra Swan	• •		...	.. ..	
☐ Trumpeter Swan	I.II	I.I.I	IIII		
☐ Mute Swan* [I]			••••		
☐ Greater White-fronted Goose	I.I.	...	.I.		
☐ Snow Goose	• ••	o	...	.. ..	
☐ Ross's Goose [A]	o		o?o	o o o ? o	
☐ Emperor Goose [R]	• ••		• ••	•• .. •• .. •• .. • .. •• ..	
☐ Canada Goose*	IIIII	I.I.	IIIII		
☐ Brant	...	...	...	.. ..	
☐ Mallard*	IIIII	I.III			
☐ American Black Duck* [I] [L]			o o	.. ..	
☐ Gadwall*	I.I.	• •	I.II		
☐ Green-winged Teal*	I.I.	I.I.	IIII		
☐ American Wigeon*	I.I.	I.I	IIII		
☐ Eurasian Wigeon	. ..		.	. . .	
☐ Northern Pintail*	IIII	I.I.	IIII		
☐ Northern Shoveler*	I.I.	• •	I.II		
☐ Blue-winged Teal*	..	...	I.II	.. ..	
☐ Garganey [A]	?		o	o o ? o	
☐ Cinnamon Teal*	...	..	I.I.	. .. .. • .	
☐ Ruddy Duck*	oo	o	I.II	.. ..	
☐ Fulvous Whistling-Duck [A]	o			o	
☐ Wood Duck*	II		IIII.	.. ..	
☐ Canvasback	. ..			.. . ? . ..	
☐ Redhead	o o	o	• ••	.. ..	
☐ Ring-necked Duck*	....	•	I.III	.. ..	
☐ Tufted Duck [R]			o	.. ..	
☐ Greater Scaup	I.III	I.II	IIII		
☐ Lesser Scaup	. ..		I.II		
☐ Common Eider [A]	o			o	
☐ King Eider [A]	o		oo	o o o o	
☐ Steller's Eider [A]	?		o	o o o ? ?	
☐ Black Scoter	I.II	....	IIII	.. ..	

SPECIES	1	2	3	CALENDAR J F M A M J J A S O N D	√
☐ White-winged Scoter					
☐ Surf Scoter					
☐ Harlequin Duck*					
☐ Oldsquaw					
☐ Barrow's Goldeneye					
☐ Common Goldeneye*					
☐ Bufflehead*					
☐ Common Merganser*					
☐ Red-breasted Merganser					
☐ Hooded Merganser*					
RAILS & COOTS					
☐ Virginia Rail*					
☐ Sora*					
☐ American Coot*					
OYSTERCATCHERS					
☐ Black Oystercatcher*					
STILTS & AVOCETS					
☐ American Avocet [R]					
☐ Black-necked Stilt [R]					
PLOVERS					
☐ Snowy Plover [R]					
☐ Semipalmated Plover					
☐ Killdeer*					
☐ Mongolian Plover [A]					
☐ Black-bellied Plover					
☐ American Golden-Plover					
☐ Pacific Golden-Plover					
SANDPIPERS					
☐ Marbled Godwit					
☐ Bar-tailed Godwit [A]					
☐ Hudsonian Godwit [A]					
☐ Bristle-thighed Curlew [A]					
☐ Whimbrel					
☐ Long-billed Curlew [R]					
☐ Willet [R]					
☐ Greater Yellowlegs					
☐ Lesser Yellowlegs					
☐ Solitary Sandpiper					
☐ Spotted Sandpiper*					
☐ Terek Sandpiper [A]					
☐ Wandering Tattler					
☐ Wilson's Phalarope* [R]					

SPECIES	1	2	3	CALENDAR J F M A M J J A S O N D	√
☐ Red-necked Phalarope					
☐ Red Phalarope			••••		
☐ Short-billed Dowitcher					
☐ Long-billed Dowitcher					
☐ Stilt Sandpiper	oo				
☐ Common Snipe*					
☐ Ruddy Turnstone					
☐ Black Turnstone					
☐ Surfbird					
☐ Rock Sandpiper			••••		
☐ Red Knot			•••		
☐ Dunlin					
☐ Sanderling					
☐ Curlew Sandpiper [A]	o		o	o o ?	
☐ Semipalmated Sandpiper					
☐ Western Sandpiper					
☐ Least Sandpiper					
☐ White-rumped Sandpiper [H]				? ? ?	
☐ Baird's Sandpiper					
☐ Sharp-tailed Sandpiper [R]	••		••	?	
☐ Pectoral Sandpiper					
☐ Ruff [R]	o		oo		
☐ Upland Sandpiper [R]	oo		••	?	
☐ Buff-breasted Sandpiper [R]	••		?••	?	
SKUA & JAEGERS					
☐ South Polar Skua		•	o		
☐ Pomarine Jaeger			•••		
☐ Parasitic Jaeger					
☐ Long-tailed Jaeger			••		
GULLS & TERNS					
☐ Heermann's Gull			••		
☐ Franklin's Gull	•••	o	•		
☐ Bonaparte's Gull					
☐ Black-headed Gull [R]			o		
☐ Little Gull			o		
☐ Ross's Gull [A]				o o	
☐ Ring-billed Gull		••			
☐ Mew Gull*					
☐ Herring Gull					
☐ California Gull					
☐ Glaucous Gull					
☐ Iceland Gull (Thayer's in part) [R]					
☐ Thayer's Gull				? ?	

SPECIES	1	2	3	CALENDAR	✓
				J F M A M J J A S O N D	
☐ Slaty-backed Gull [A]	o			o o o ... o	
☐ Western Gull*	▥	▥	...		
☐ Glaucous-winged Gull*	▥	▥	▥		
☐ Black-legged Kittiwake	▥	..	....		
☐ Sabine's Gull	▥.	....	•••		
☐ Common Tern	oo	.	▥		
☐ Arctic Tern	··ı		o		
☐ Forster's Tern [A]				o o o	
☐ Black Tern [A]	o?			? o ?	
☐ Elegant Tern [R]	•		o		
☐ Caspian Tern	ı·	ı·	ı·		
AUKS & PUFFINS					
☐ Common Murre*	▥	▥	▥		
☐ Thick-billed Murre [R] [L]	oo			o o o o	
☐ Pigeon Guillemot*	▥	▥	▥		
☐ Marbled Murrelet*	▥	▥	▥		
☐ Kittlitz's Murrelet [A]				o o o o o o	
☐ Xantus's Murrelet [A]	oo			o o	
☐ Ancient Murrelet	.ı	ı	...		
☐ Cassin's Auklet*	▥	....	oooo		
☐ Parakeet Auklet [R]	• ••			•• •• •• ••• ••	
☐ Crested Auklet [H] Δ	?			? ? ?	
☐ Rhinoceros Auklet*	▥.	ıll·	▥·		
☐ Horned Puffin [R]	• ·		••		
☐ Tufted Puffin*	▥.	...	oo		
AMERICAN VULTURES					
☐ Turkey Vulture*	....	·ı	▥·		
KITES, EAGLES & HAWKS					
☐ Golden Eagle*	....	....	....		
☐ Bald Eagle*	▥	▥	▥		
☐ White-tailed Kite [H]			? ?	o ? o	
☐ Northern Harrier*	..	·ı	ıll		
☐ Sharp-shinned Hawk*	▥	ıll	▥		
☐ Cooper's Hawk* (L west coast)	·ı.	·ı	▥		
☐ Northern Goshawk*	....	....	....		
☐ Broad-winged Hawk [R] [L]			?	? ••• •	
☐ Red-tailed Hawk*	▥	▥	▥		
☐ Swainson's Hawk [R]			••••	• •• •• •• •• • •• •• ••	
☐ Rough-legged Hawk	o o		· ..		
OSPREY					
☐ Osprey*	▥ı	▥ı	▥·		

SPECIES	1	2	3	CALENDAR J F M A M J J A S O N D	√
FALCONS					
☐ American Kestrel*	....	.. ..	.·.·	.. .·.. .. ·.. ..	
☐ Merlin*	·II·	·I·I·	IIIII	.· .·.. ·.	
☐ Prairie Falcon [A]	?			? o ?	
☐ Peregrine Falcon*	I·II	I·II·	I·I·I	.· .·.. .. .·.. ..	
☐ Gyrfalcon	••		·..	.. ·.. .· ·.. ..	
GROUSE & PTARMIGAN					
☐ Ruffed Grouse*	IIIII	IIIII	IIIII		
☐ Blue Grouse*	IIIII	IIIII	IIIII	▬▬▬▬	
☐ White-tailed Ptarmigan*	IIIII		....		
☐ California Quail* [I]		I...	IIIII	▬▬▬▬	
☐ Mountain Quail* [I] [X?]				.. ·.. .. ·.. ..	
☐ Gray Partridge* [X]				• • • • • • • • • • • •	
☐ Ring-necked Pheasant* [I]			IIIII		
☐ Wild Turkey* [I] [NC]				.. .· ..	
PIGEONS & DOVES					
☐ Band-tailed Pigeon*	III·	III·		.· ▬▬▬	
☐ Rock Dove* [I] [L west coast]	....	e		▬▬▬▬▬▬	
☐ Mourning Dove* [L]	....	·. ..	....	.. ·.. .. .·.. ..	
☐ White-winged Dove [A]	oo	o		o o o o	
CUCKOOS					
☐ Yellow-billed Cuckoo [A]				o o	
OWLS					
☐ Barn Owl* [L]			....	.. .· ..	
☐ Short-eared Owl*	·.·.	•	·.I	.. .· .. .·	
☐ Long-eared Owl*	o		····	·· ·· ·. • .· ·· ··	
☐ Great Horned Owl*	IIII	IIII	IIIII		
☐ Barred Owl*	o	o	IIIII		
☐ Great Gray Owl [A]	o		o o	o o o	
☐ Snowy Owl	··	••	I·II	·· ·· .. ··	
☐ Western Screech-Owl*	IIIII	IIIII	IIIII		
☐ Northern Pygmy-Owl*	IIIII	IIIII	IIIII	.· .· ·. ··	
☐ Northern Saw-whet Owl*	·.·.		I.I	.· .· ·. ··	
☐ Northern Hawk-Owl [A]			o	o o o	
☐ Boreal Owl [A]	oo		o	o o o	
☐ Burrowing Owl [R]			• ••	·· ·· ·· • ·· ·· ··	
NIGHTJARS					
☐ Common Poorwill [A]				o	
☐ Common Nighthawk*	·I·	I·	I·	▬▬▬ ··	
SWIFTS					
☐ Black Swift*	III	·I·	III	H ··▬·▬·▬· . H	
☐ Vaux's Swift*	III	I·I·	III	·· ·▬·▬·	

SPECIES	1	2	3	CALENDAR (J F M A M J J A S O N D)	√
HUMMINGBIRDS					
☐ Costa's Hummingbird [A]			oo		
☐ Anna's Hummingbird* [L]	....	o	...		
☐ Calliope Hummingbird [A]			?		
☐ Rufous Hummingbird*	IIII	IIII	IIII .		
☐ Allen's Hummingbird [H]					
KINGFISHERS					
☐ Belted Kingfisher*	IIIII	IIIII	IIIII		
WOODPECKERS					
☐ Northern Flicker*	IIIII	IIIII	IIIII		
☐ Lewis's Woodpecker* [R]			ooo		
☐ Red-breasted Sapsucker*	..ııl	..ııl	IIIII		
☐ Red-naped Sapsucker* [R]			.		
☐ Yellow-bellied Sapsucker [A]			o o		
☐ Downy Woodpecker*	IIIII	IIIII	IIIII		
☐ Hairy Woodpecker*	IIIII	IIIII	IIIII		
☐ Three-toed Woodpecker* [R]	....		• ••		
☐ Pileated Woodpecker*	ıııll	ıııll	IIIII		
FLYCATCHERS					
☐ Eastern Kingbird*	..	.	...		
☐ Gray Kingbird [A]	o				
☐ Thick-billed Kingbird [A]			o		
☐ Western Kingbird	...	...	... ?		
☐ Tropical Kingbird [R]		••	o		
☐ Scissor-tailed Flycatcher [A]	o?		?		
☐ Great Crested Flycatcher [A]	o				
☐ Ash-throated Flycatcher [R]	oo		oo		
☐ Olive-sided Flycatcher*	II.	II.	III.		
☐ Western Wood-Pewee*	...	..	ıll		
☐ Say's Phoebe [R]	ooo		••		
☐ Dusky Flycatcher [A]			o		
☐ Hammond's Flycatcher*	ııll	...	III.		
☐ Least Flycatcher* [A]			o		
☐ Willow Flycatcher*					
☐ Pacific-slope Flycatcher*	IIII		IIIII		
LARKS					
☐ Sky Lark* [I]	o				
☐ Horned Lark*	o o	•	..|.		
SWALLOWS					
☐ Tree Swallow*	II.	..	II.		
☐ Violet-green Swallow*	II.	III.	II.		
☐ Purple Martin* [L]	o		...		

SPECIES	1	2	3	CALENDAR
				J F M A M J J A S O N D
☐ Bank Swallow				
☐ N. Rough-winged Swallow*				
☐ Cliff Swallow* [L west coast]				
☐ Barn Swallow*				
JAYS & CROWS				
☐ Blue Jay [R]				
☐ Steller's Jay*				
☐ Gray Jay*				
☐ Clark's Nutcracker [R]				
☐ Black-billed Magpie [R]				
☐ Northwestern Crow*				
☐ Common Raven*				
CHICKADEES				
☐ Black-capped Chickadee [H]				
☐ Mountain Chickadee [H]				
☐ Chestnut-backed Chickadee*				
BUSHTITS				
☐ Bushtit* [L west coast]				
CREEPERS & NUTHATCHES				
☐ Brown Creeper*				
☐ White-breasted Nuthatch [A]				
☐ Red-breasted Nuthatch*				
☐ Pygmy Nuthatch [A]				
WRENS				
☐ House Wren*				
☐ Winter Wren*				
☐ Bewick's Wren* [L west coast]				
☐ Marsh Wren*				
☐ Rock Wren* [R]				
KINGLETS & THRUSHES				
☐ Golden-crowned Kinglet*				
☐ Ruby-crowned Kinglet*				
☐ Blue-gray Gnatcatcher [A]				
☐ Western Bluebird*				
☐ Mountain Bluebird				
☐ Townsend's Solitaire*				
☐ Veery [A]				
☐ Swainson's Thrush*				
☐ Hermit Thrush*				
☐ Varied Thrush*				
☐ American Robin*				
☐ Northern Wheatear [A]				

SPECIES	1	2	3	J	F	M	A	M	J	J	A	S	O	N	D	√
SHRIKES																
☐ Loggerhead Shrike [A]										o						
☐ Northern Shrike	.?..	..	⊔⊔										.			
MIMIC THRUSHES																
☐ Gray Catbird [A]			∞ o				o		o	o		?		o	o	
☐ Northern Mockingbird* [R]	....	o	....	..	..	..	..	..	..	..	..	..	..	..	..	
☐ Sage Thrasher [A]	o								o							
☐ Brown Thrasher [A]	o		∞					o	o				o			
PIPITS & WAGTAILS																
☐ American Pipit*	⊔⊔	.	⊔⊔⊔					..	..	..	..	▬				
☐ Red-throated Pipit [A]	?												o	o	?	
☐ Black-backed Wagtail [A]	o								o							
☐ wagtail species † [A]	†	†								††			†			
☐ Yellow Wagtail [A]													o	o		
DIPPER																
☐ American Dipper*	⊔⊔⊔	....	⊔⊔⊔⊔													
WAXWINGS																
☐ Bohemian Waxwing	o?oo		. .	..	..	..	..	?				..	..	..	..	
☐ Cedar Waxwing*	⊔⊔⊔.	⊔⊔⊔.	⊔⊔⊔.	..	..	..	..	.	▬▬▬▬▬▬							
STARLINGS & MYNA																
☐ Crested Myna* [I]			••••	Ɵ	Ɵ	Ɵ	Ɵ	Ɵ	Ɵ	Ɵ	Ɵ	Ɵ	Ɵ	Ɵ	Ɵ	
☐ European Starling* [I] [X]	⊔⊔⊔⊔	⊔⊔⊔⊔	⊔⊔⊔⊔	▬▬▬▬▬▬▬▬▬▬▬▬												
WARBLERS & VIREOS																
☐ Hutton's Vireo*	....	⊔⊔⊔⊔	⊔⊔⊔.													
☐ Cassin's Vireo*	...	•	⊔⊔				..	▬▬▬▬			.					
☐ Red-eyed Vireo*	...	•	.					.	▬▬▬		.					
☐ Warbling Vireo*	⊔⊔⊔⊔	⊔⊔⊔⊔	⊔⊔⊔⊔			.	▬▬▬▬▬▬			.						
☐ Tennessee Warbler [A]	?		???	?	?		?	o	?		?	?		?		
☐ Orange-crowned Warbler*	⊔⊔⊔.	⊔⊔⊔.	⊔⊔⊔.	..	..	▬▬▬▬▬▬▬						..	..			
☐ Nashville Warbler [R]	••••	o	••••	••		••	••	?	?	••	••	••	••			
☐ Northern Parula [A]			o										o			
☐ Black-and-white Warbler [A]	?			?			?		?	?		o				
☐ Chestnut-sided Warbler [H]	?		?							?		?				
☐ Magnolia Warbler [A]			oooo					o	o	o	o	o			o	
☐ Yellow-rumped Warbler*	⊔⊔⊔.	⊔⊔.	⊔⊔⊔.	..	..	.	▬▬▬▬▬▬▬									
☐ Black-throated Gray Warbler*	..	⊔.	⊔⊔⊔.	.	..	▬▬▬▬▬						..	.	?		
☐ Townsend's Warbler*	⊔⊔.	⊔⊔.	⊔⊔⊔.	..	..	▬▬▬▬▬▬						..	..			
☐ Hermit Warbler [A]	?		∞				o	o	o							
☐ Prairie Warbler [A]	o											o				
☐ Bay-breasted Warbler [A]	o											o				
☐ Yellow-throated Warbler [A]			o	o												
☐ Blackpoll Warbler [A]	? o							o	?		o	o				

SPECIES	1	2	3	CALENDAR (J F M A M J J A S O N D)	√
☐ Palm Warbler	· ··	··	··		
☐ Yellow Warbler*	‖‖·				
☐ MacGillivray's Warbler*	‖‖·				
☐ Canada Warbler [A]		o			o
☐ Wilson's Warbler*	‖‖‖	‖‖‖	‖‖‖		
☐ Hooded Warbler [A]	o				o
☐ Northern Waterthrush [R] [L]			oo	o o ··o o o	
☐ Common Yellowthroat*	‖‖‖	‖‖·	‖‖‖		
☐ Yellow-breasted Chat [A]	o		oo	o o o	
☐ American Redstart [A]	oo		oo	o ? o o o	
GROSBEAKS & SPARROWS					
☐ Rose-breasted Grosbeak [A]	o oo		o	o o o o o o o o	
☐ Black-headed Grosbeak*	·.·?	..	‖‖‖	? · .. ? ?	
☐ Indigo Bunting [A]				o o o o	
☐ Lazuli Bunting*	ooɩ		··	·· ··· ·	
☐ Green-tailed Towhee [A]			o oo	o o o o o o	
☐ Spotted Towhee*	‖‖‖	‖‖‖	‖‖‖		
☐ Grasshopper Sparrow [A]		o		o o	
☐ Le Conte's Sparrow [A]			o	o	
☐ Vesper Sparrow* [L]	o		‖‖‖		
☐ Savannah Sparrow*	‖·‖·	‖‖·	‖‖‖		
☐ Song Sparrow*	‖‖‖	‖‖‖	‖‖‖		
☐ Lark Sparrow [R]	····		···	· · ··· ·· ·· · · ·· ··	
☐ Black-throated Sparrow [A]				o	
☐ Sage Sparrow [A]				o	
☐ American Tree Sparrow	o oo		· ··		
☐ Chipping Sparrow*	oo				
☐ Clay-colored Sparrow [A]	o			? o o	
☐ Brewer's Sparrow [A]				o	
☐ Dark-eyed Junco*	‖‖‖	‖‖‖	‖‖‖		
☐ Harris's Sparrow	· ··		.? ..	·· ·· ·· · ? ?	
☐ White-throated Sparrow	· ··		‖·‖		
☐ White-crowned Sparrow*	‖·‖	‖·‖	‖‖‖		
☐ Golden-crowned Sparrow*	‖·‖	‖·‖·	‖·‖·		
☐ Fox Sparrow*	‖‖‖	‖‖‖	‖‖‖		
☐ Lincoln's Sparrow*	‖·‖·	‖·‖·	‖·‖		
☐ Swamp Sparrow	··	··	? ..	·· ··· · ?	
☐ Chestnut-collared Longspur [A]	o		o	o o	
☐ Smith's Longspur [A]				? o ?	
☐ Lapland Longspur	· ‖·	·	‖· ‖·	·· · ·· ··	
☐ Snow Bunting	··	·	·· ..	·· ··· ··	
☐ McKay's Bunting [A]	o			o	
☐ Rustic Bunting [A]	o o	oo		o o o o o o	

SPECIES	1	2	3	CALENDAR J F M A M J J A S O N D	√
☐ Dickcissel [A]	oo			o · · o o · · o · o o ·	
☐ Lark Bunting [A]				o	
BLACKBIRDS					
☐ Bobolink* [R]	o		o	·· ·· ··	
☐ Western Meadowlark*	·· ‚	··· ‚	‚·ıl‚	·· ·· ·· ·· ··	
☐ Yellow-headed Blackbird	oo	····	· ·· ·· ·· ·· ·· ·· ··	
☐ Red-winged Blackbird*	l‚ıı	l‚ıı	‖‖‖		
☐ Rusty Blackbird	? o		· ··	·· ·· ·· ? ·· ·· ··	
☐ Brewer's Blackbird* [L west c.]	··		‖‖‖		
☐ Brown-headed Cowbird*	‖·	‖·	▬▬▬	
☐ Common Grackle [A]	o ?		o	o o o o o o o o o	
☐ Bullock's Oriole*	····	·	ıl	·· ·· ·· ·· ·· · ··	
☐ Baltimore Oriole [A]		?		o o o o o ? o o	
☐ Hooded Oriole [A]				o o	
☐ Scarlet Tanager [A]			o	o	
☐ Western Tanager*	···	‚··	‖l‚	· ·· ▬■▬ ·· ·· ··	
WEAVERS					
☐ House Sparrow* [I] [L west c.]	ıııı	‚ııı	‖‖‖		
FINCHES					
☐ Pine Siskin*	‖‖‖	‖ı‚	‖‖‖		
☐ American Goldfinch*	‖‖‖	‖l·	l‚ıı	▬▬▬	
☐ Red Crossbill*	‖‖‖	‖ıı	‖‖‖	▬▬	
☐ White-winged Crossbill [R]	····	o	····	o o o o o o	
☐ Pine Grosbeak	··· ‚		··· ‚	·· ·· ·· · ? ·· ·· ··	
☐ Common Redpoll [R]	? o		oo	·· o o o ? o o	
☐ Gray-crowned Rosy Finch [R]	····		oooo	·· · ·· ·· ··	
☐ Purple Finch*	ıllı	‖l·	‖‖‖		
☐ Cassin's Finch [A]			o	o	
☐ House Finch* [L west coast]	·ıl	·‚ ··	▬▬▬		
☐ Evening Grosbeak*	‚ılı	‚ıı‚	‖‖‖		
☐ Brambling [A]	o o		o o	o o o o o o o	

¥ Photograph required: As identification of frigatebird species is problematical, the possibility of a Great or Lesser Frigatebird being involved (though inconsequential) cannot be ignored.

Δ Old specimen which may have been collected too far offshore for inclusion to Canada list.

All records from Rocky Point Bird Banding Station are considered hypothetical unless confirmed with photographs.

HYPOTHETICAL SPECIES	1	2	3	J	F	M	A	M	J	J	A	S	O	N	D	√
☐ Manx Shearwater	? ?									?		?				
☐ Streaked Shearwater	?										?					
☐ Murphy's Petrel	?					?										
☐ Whooper Swan [origin?]*			o ?									o		?		
☐ Falcated Duck [origin?]	o o			o	o	o	o									
☐ Smew								?					?			
☐ Little Curlew	?												?			
☐ Red-necked Stint											?					
☐ Ivory Gull						?										
☐ Oriental Turtle-Dove [origin?]	o											o				
☐ Ruby-throated Hummingbird		?							?							
☐ Black-chinned Hummingbird	?	?							?	?		?				
☐ Dusky Thrush	?													?		
☐ Phainopepla											?					
☐ Black-throated Green Warbler			??					?	?			?				
☐ Mourning Warbler													?			
☐ Connecticut Warbler	?												?			
☐ Ovenbird													?			
* origin highly suspect																

Explanation of Symbols

Status

The following symbols depict the probability of an individual to see at least one bird in appropriate habitat at the correct season.

▬▬▬▬▬	Hard to miss
▬▬▬▬	Should see
▬▬▬	May see
·············	How lucky can you get
●	Vagrant (not recorded annually)
o	Accidental (fewer than 10 records)
·	Rare (recorded in low numbers)

Symbols

*	Nesting (one successful breeding record)
[A]	Accidental
[R]	Rare
[H]	Hypothetical (well-documented: requires photos)
[SR]	Sight record (written descriptions by few observers)
?	Questionable record (not well documented)
[I]	Introduced (successfully established for 10 years plus)
[NC]	Not countable (introduced species not established)
[X]e	Extripated (species has vanished in modern times)
[L]	Local (populations confined to localized sites)
[origin?]	Possible aviary escapee

CALENDAR
J-F-M-A-M-J-J-A-S-O-N-D

J - January   F - February

M - March   A - April   etc.

LOCALITIES

[1] Western & Northwestern

[2] Southwest Coast

[3] Central East Coast

[4] Southern Vancouver Island

SEASON

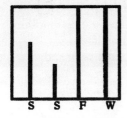

S   Spring   March - May

S   Summer   June - August

F   Fall   September - November

W   Winter   December - February

HOW TO USE THE BAR-GRAPHS

The first step is to consult your National Geographic's *Field Guide to the Birds of North America,* whose maps indicate which species range on Vancouver Island, and if they occur in summer, winter, or as a resident (unfortunately migration routes are not depicted!). If you are interested as to the exact arrival and departure dates, refer to the calendar and bar-graphs. The first three columns represent the Island as divided into three biogeoclimatic zones (see Localities & Map). Each of these three columns is divided into spring, summer, fall, and winter. A line spanning the box from top-to-bottom represents that the species is common at that season, while a line of variable length indicates a status from fairly common (longest) to fairly rare (shortest). A small dot indicates that the species is rare at that season, while a [•] or [o] represents a vagrant or an accidental species. Species marked thus * (169) indicates that the species has nested on the Island.

The next twelve columns represents the calendar year with the seasonal occurrence and relative abundance centered on the fourth and most important biogeoclimatic zone which has the greatest bird diversity on the Island; Southern Vancouver Island. The placement of bars within the calendar year show the exact arrival and departure dates for migrants, while the varying widths of bars show the relative abundance of the species. Although the calendar represents the status of birds on Southern Vancouver Island, all vagrants and accidental records are presented from the entire Island and also displayed on the calendar. Migrants arrive and depart on similar dates throughout much of Vancouver Island, while the seasonal status and relative abundance varies greatly—especially between the east and west coasts. If you are not birding on Southern Vancouver Island check the first three columns for the species status in the region you are birding. Example: Double-crested Cormorant displays a "Hard to Miss" bar across the calendar as it is a common species throughout the year somewhere on the Island. However, in columns [1] and [2] it is shown as rare there during summer, etc. The status of pelagics noted on the calendar is significantly different from the West Coast. Example: Black-footed Albatross is blank across the calendar as it has not been recorded on Southern Vancouver Island, accidental in column [3], but column [1] displays the West Coast pelagic status, uncommon during spring, summer, fall, and rare in winter. The status of storm-petrels and breeding alcids is noted by chance of seeing them on pelagic trips. (See *Checklist of British Columbia Birds* which has the pelagics arrival and departure dates displayed on the calendar.)

Scoter
  Black 8, 13, 26, 31, 61,
    86, 93, 95, 97, 115,
    118, 123, 129, 138
  Surf 8, 26, 31, 47, 61,
    68, 70, 88, 91, 92, 93,
    95, 104, 110, 112,
    115, 123, 129, 139
  White-winged 8, 13, 26,
    31, 47, 61, 68, 70, 91,
    92, 93, 95, 115, 123,
    129, 130, 139
Shearwater
  Black-vented 18, 109,
    137
  Buller's 2, 18, 109, 137
  Flesh-footed 18, 109,
    137
  Manx 148
  Pink-footed 18, 109, 137
  Short-tailed 18, 21, 47,
    109, 137
  Sooty 18, 20, 47, 108,
    109, 112, 130, 137
  Streaked 148
Shoveler
  Northern 9, 11, 13, 14,
    32, 51, 61, 76, 80,
    93, 105, 122, 138
Shrike
  Loggerhead 32, 145
  Northern 11, 26, 31,
    32, 60, 76, 88, 96,
    101, 103, 117,
    145
Siskin
  Pine 50, 61, 64, 69, 74,
    82, 86, 90, 96, 103,
    120, 125, 129, 134,
    147

Skua
  South Polar 2, 19, 109,
    140
Smew 148

Snipe
  Common 29, 32, 41, 52,
    53, 72, 80, 89, 91, 95,
    102, 105, 117, 140
Solitaire
  Townsend's 34, 38, 40,
    41, 54, 64, 78, 101,
    144
Sora 11, 13, 51, 80, 86,
    90, 123, 139
Sparrow
  American Tree 31, 146
  Black-throated 38, 146
  Brewer's 50, 146
  Chipping 11, 13, 40,
    51, 52, 53, 86, 87,
    89, 96, 119, 146
  Clay-colored 110, 146
  Fox 16, 26, 32, 39, 43,
    49, 60, 64, 67, 69,
    80, 90, 91, 96, 108,
    111, 133, 135, 146
  Golden-crowned 9, 13,
    26, 30, 31, 32, 39, 41,
    43, 49, 61, 66, 67, 69,
    80, 88, 91, 96, 113,
    146
  Grasshopper 29, 33,
    50, 67, 146
  Harris's 11, 30, 146
  House 11, 13, 18, 61,
    96, 147
  Lark 38, 40, 110, 146
  Le Conte's 146
  Lincoln's 30, 31, 32,
    39, 43, 49, 50, 51, 52,
    66, 93, 96, 121, 146
  Sage 146
  Savannah 18, 29, 30,
    31, 32, 40, 43, 69,
    86, 88, 96, 105, 119,
    121, 124, 146
  Song 18, 26, 31, 34, 38,
    49, 53, 60, 64, 67,
    69, 80, 82, 86, 90,

91, 96, 103, 105,
    110, 111, 112, 113,
    120, 125, 129, 131,
    134, 146
  Swamp 11, 49, 50, 51,
    52, 67, 80, 146
  Vesper 11, 75, 84, 85,
    146
  White-crowned 13, 31,
    39, 49, 53, 61, 67,
    69, 74, 82, 87, 88,
    96, 103, 112, 113,
    119, 134, 146
  White-throated 11, 41,
    49, 67, 146
Starling
  European 18, 69, 82,
    96, 122, 145
Stilt
  Black-necked 9, 45,
    121, 139
Stint
  Little 9
  Red-necked 9, 148
  Temmincies 9
Storm-Petrel
  Fork-tailed 14, 18, 20,
    22, 47, 101, 109, 137
  Leach's 14, 18, 21, 47,
    109, 121, 137
Surfbird 2, 9, 42, 44, 45,
    48, 60, 95, 101, 115,
    140
Swallow
  Bank 10, 33, 47, 76,
    122, 144
  Barn 10, 18, 66, 68, 86,
    90, 96, 103, 115,
    119, 122, 135, 144
  Cliff 10, 13, 51, 89, 90,
    96,144
  Northern Rough-winged
    33, 55, 68, 75, 90,
    112, 115, 119, 122,
    133, 135,144

ABOUT THE AUTHOR

Keith began his interest in birds as a boy growing up in Saskatchewan and Ontario. Immigrating to Australia, he worked as a field researcher studying the distribution of Queensland's rainforest birds. Returning to Victoria, where he continues to reside, Keith joined the staff of the Royal British Columbia Museum as curator of ornithological collections and as illustrator. During his stay he embellished a plethora of scientific papers and journals and a series of handbooks on the province's birds, reptiles and amphibians with his drawings.

Recently, Keith has been self-employed as a freelance water-colour artist and has published birding guides to Costa Rica, Thailand, Malaysia, Ecuador, British Columbia, Vancouver Island and the two CD-ROM's advertised on this web page, *A Birder's Guide to Costa Rica* and *Observing 900 Species in North America*. He has also written numerous articles for birding and natural history magazines and has led birding tours including co-leading with Wings Inc..

Semi-retired, Keith has been touring the world with birding trips, among others, to Hawaii, Costa Rica, Jamaica, Tahiti, South Africa, Great Britain and Mexico. North America's birding hotspots still hold his most intense interest and Keith holds the highest ABA list of any Canadian—750 species.

Visit Keith Taylor's website at
http://members.home.net/birdersguide